Praise for

ALREADY ENOUGH

"In these pages, Lisa Olivera explains how to change the stories we tell ourselves about ourselves. With small shifts in our thinking, she shows that we can experience tremendous healing. She lights the way down what was once a dark road. *Already Enough* is beautiful, meditative, touching. and hopeful."

—Arianna Huffington, founder & CEO, Thrive Global

"This collection of work is wrapped in truth and vulnerability. Each page creates a sense of soulful reverence."

—Alexandra Elle, author of *After the Rain*

"*Already Enough* is a balm for all of us for whom false stories have ruled our lives and limited our vision. Lisa Olivera's *Already Enough* empowers readers by offering a path to liberation from the stories that have limited us for long enough. Part memoir, part guide, and all heart, *Already Enough* is a must-read for anyone searching for their true story underneath the false and often toxic narratives that no longer serve them."

—Christie Tate, author of *New York Times* bestseller *Group*

"We all come with stories but have you ever wondered about yours? Is it true? Does it define me? *Already Enough* by Lisa Olivera is a template to help us uncover the true nature of ourselves. Thought-provoking, touching, and supportive, a book for all who have ever thought they might not be good enough."

—Sharon Salzberg, author of *Lovingkindness* and
Real Change

"*Already Enough* is an insightful, deeply personal journey into self-compassion and self-acceptance. Authenticity shines through every page, as readers are invited to find their own pathway to the realization that they are already enough."

—Kristin Neff, author of *Self-Compassion* and
Fierce Self-Compassion

"With honesty and grace Lisa offers a beautiful roadmap for transformation. She reminds us again and again that no matter what our current circumstances, and no matter what has happened in the past, healing is always possible."

—Shauna Shapiro, PhD, professor and author of
Good Morning, I Love You

"An insightful, compassionate therapist offers practical, positive advice, and self-help strategies for reframing painful life stories."

—*Shelf Awareness*

ALREADY ENOUGH

A PATH TO SELF-ACCEPTANCE

LISA OLIVERA

SIMON & SCHUSTER PAPERBACKS

NEW YORK   LONDON   TORONTO   SYDNEY   NEW DELHI

Simon & Schuster Paperbacks
An Imprint of Simon & Schuster, Inc.
1230 Avenue of the Americas
New York, NY 10020

First Simon & Schuster trade paperback edition January 2023

SIMON & SCHUSTER PAPERBACKS and colophon
are registered trademarks of Simon & Schuster, Inc.

For information about special discounts for bulk purchases, please contact
Simon & Schuster Special Sales at 1-866-506-1949 or business@simonandschuster.com.

The Simon & Schuster Speakers Bureau can bring authors to your live event.
For more information or to book an event, contact the
Simon & Schuster Speakers Bureau at 1-866-248-3049 or
visit our website at www.simonspeakers.com.

Interior design by Ruth Lee-Mui

Manufactured in the United States of America

1   3   5   7   9   10   8   6   4   2

Library of Congress Cataloging-in-Publication Data has been applied for.

ISBN 978-1-9821-3892-9
ISBN 978-1-9821-8267-0 (pbk)
ISBN 978-1-9821-3895-0 (ebook)

For everyone doing the difficult, beautiful work
of remembering who you truly are.

Contents

PART ONE

GETTING HONEST

My Story—and Your Story

On Mother's Day in 1987, when I was a few hours old, I was abandoned behind a rock near Muir Woods in Northern California. I was wrapped in a blue blanket, with no other evidence of where I had come from. I was found by a man and woman who were out bird-watching with their toddler. They called an ambulance to take me to the nearest emergency room. I was determined to be healthy, with no signs of distress other than sunburn. Two days later, another couple who would become my parents took me home.

Growing up, I knew I was adopted. I later discovered I was abandoned and, despite having loving parents, knowing all this about myself led to a lot of pain—pain I didn't want anyone to see. Pain that I ignored for decades. I spent years longing to understand where I came from. Not knowing my birth family was at times excruciating. I hated getting assigned family trees in school. I hated getting told I looked like one of my parents. I hated hearing my friends talk about things they'd inherited from family members. And most of all, I hated that I hated it. I was told to feel lucky, to feel grateful, to feel happy, but a lot of the time, I just felt sad.

I looked for myself in strangers and often wondered about who my birth mother was and why she had abandoned me in the woods. I imagined my birth mother out there, somewhere. I watched random women with dark hair and blue eyes, like my own, thinking maybe they could be her. Without realizing it, I formed what would grow into a deeply held belief: I was not enough as I was. Something was wrong with me. Why else had I been left to die?

To answer that question, I began to tell myself a story: I would never be loved or even accepted as who I was because I was not enough as I was. This story wasn't true, but it made sense of an experience that deeply confused me. It allowed me to move forward with a sense of control over an experience I had no say in. It sounds dramatic, but it felt like the only way.

I lived in that story for years; it permeated every aspect of my life. I didn't believe I could possibly be myself because I hadn't been wanted from the start. I tried to avoid my way out of it; I hesitated to seek out new friends, thinking, somehow, they would discover that I was not enough. I tried to perfect my way out of it; I strived to be as special and talented and unique and smart as possible, thinking *that* would make me enough. It wasn't until a suicide attempt at age fourteen that I finally began, through therapy and healing practices, exploring my story, and how it affected my identity and my relationship to myself and to others.

Doing so felt terrifying and overwhelming. I didn't know if my story was something I could actually change. These things weren't taught to me or talked about when I was growing up, so I had no idea what was possible. I realized, though, that in order to have the chance of living a life as my full self, I needed to confront my story, explore it, and rewrite it.

I sat on a therapist's couch week after week and began the process of examining the belief I had formed and the story that unfolded from it. My therapist specialized in working with adoptees, so it didn't take a lot of explaining for her to truly understand the pain I was carrying. She really saw me; I could tell by the feeling in my chest that always seemed to loosen a bit while I was in her office. I remember her saying, "Lots of adoptees feel this way—lots of adoptees feel like they weren't enough and still aren't. You are not alone, and it's okay to feel this way. We can move through it slowly." I felt such a deep sense of relief, knowing I wasn't the only one. I had never connected with other adoptees, so hearing this gave me a feeling of community—even with people I had never met.

Sharing my truth with a therapist was the catalyst for giving myself permission to explore my story. I had never put words to it, and finding the words to express what I was feeling inside brought clarity. Being able to speak honestly and openly about my story—which I had previously kept hidden and quiet—was freeing. That experience put me on a path of lifelong healing and growth, and it has been difficult—but it ultimately reminded me that I have more control over my story than I had long believed. We all do.

While I hold many titles, one of my current roles is a therapist who supports clients in untangling their stories. I didn't always think I'd end up here, offering what I once needed. In seeing how others explored this work, though, I was able to understand what I had been feeling for so long. So many people gave me permission to explore this within myself and, in turn, within my own work. People like Brené Brown, a research professor who revolutionized the study of courage, vulnerability, empathy, shame, and—especially relevant here—owning our stories. People like Tara Brach, a psychologist who taught me so much about what she calls radical acceptance, or the idea that finding acceptance in what *is* allows us to return to our true selves. People like Carl Rogers, a psychologist who co-founded humanistic psychology and reminded us we're enough as we are. People like Pema Chödrön, Mary Oliver, bell hooks, Glennon Doyle, Sharon Salzberg, Cheryl Strayed, Irvin Yalom, Elizabeth Gilbert, and Rick Hanson, writers and thinkers, all of whom have influenced my life and work in so many different ways. Areas of study like narrative therapy, which helps us externalize a problem instead of feeling like a problem; Internal Family Systems therapy, which allows us to witness and heal all different parts that live within us; mindfulness-based therapy, which teaches us how to find more presence and nonjudgmental awareness in our lives; compassion-focused therapy, which encourages compassion toward self and others; family systems, which gives us insight into how our family of origin affects who we are; and acceptance and commitment therapy, which explores acceptance, mindfulness, and emotional flexibility. All of these various spiritual teachers, creatives, leaders, and healing modalities have informed the way I view myself and the world.

One of the most important things I have learned in my work is that I created my story for a reason: I created the story of not being enough to make sense of what happened to me. Because I didn't have answers I needed, I created answers for myself. I see this experience in clients, too. It's easy to forget that our stories are functioning for us in some way, even if they're challenging. Getting curious about what my story was doing for me, as painful as it was, gave me insight into making sense of *why* I was carrying this story. This was the beginning of my own healing journey. Clients often find that it's the beginning of theirs. I've written this book so you can start, and continue, yours.

The dictionary definition of healing is "the process of becoming sound or healthy again." We instantly understand this in the physical sense when it comes to healing from illness or injury, but it applies to our emotional health as well. The word that stands out to me here is "process," and I have deeply felt the importance of remembering it is a process as my own healing journey continues to ebb and flow while I grow in my own life—that there is no end point in healing, but instead an ebb and flow we are constantly in relationship with. All too often, healing is approached in our culture as something to achieve by a quick fix, something to check off the list.

The hard truth is this: healing—of any kind—doesn't happen overnight. It is not a one-time-only experience, it isn't linear, and it isn't something we ever totally finish. Healing doesn't mean fixing, forgetting, erasing, or undoing. Healing means integrating the painful pieces of our story so we can become more whole, so we can become our full selves. It means allowing ourselves to carry our story without being carried by it.

The beautiful truth is this: healing is always available to us, and it is always a process, which also means it is always possible. I have learned this through exploring my own story and through witnessing the stories of my clients.

Our stories—the experiences we've had and beliefs we've formed, and the narratives we've developed in *response* to those experiences and beliefs—affect us in countless ways. They affect our sense of self and our relationships. They affect the choices we make and how we take care of ourselves. They affect the lens through which we view the world and the ways we show up in it. They affect us in so many ways we don't even realize until we take a closer look . . . which is exactly why this exploration is so important.

While we tell ourselves *so* many stories, I've noticed that we tend to have one or two that we tell ourselves the loudest. When we think about those loud stories, we can often trace their origin to certain experiences or even specific moments growing up. When I think about my experience, so much of it stems back to the meaning I made of being abandoned and adopted. As a child, I created stories of not being worthy, not belonging, and needing to be as close to perfect as possible to be lovable—all because I believed I was not enough as I was.

In my practice, I've seen how other people's stories grow from that same belief. So many of us have come to believe that we are not enough as we are. That, for some reason, we have to change parts of ourselves or do certain things to be loved, heard and seen, understood and accepted. I've come to understand this belief of not being enough as a root belief.

A root belief is the central belief that informs how we feel about ourselves and the world. It is from this root belief that our sense of self, our stories about who we are, and our way of being in the world are formed. What grows from it looks different for each of us; there are many variants. For some, it might be people-pleasing in order to feel good enough; for others, it might look like denying their needs in order to be worthy of love. No matter what it looks like in your specific context, the result is the same. Everything grows from the root: when the root is harsh or critical, flourishing is difficult. When we look at our stories, we can start realizing what has grown (or not grown) from there. If our root isn't strong and healthy, we can't grow far beyond it. If the root is sturdy enough to withstand the storm, though, then we can bloom through whatever comes our way. This is why examining our stories is so critical. It brings to light what has been underneath the surface for so long and allows us to recognize how we have grown the thoughts, beliefs, and behaviors we've since experienced. From there, we get to start choosing what we water and what we let die.

We are not taught to pause and examine whether these stories are actually true or, more important, if they are actually serving us. When I work with clients, I see and hear the ahas they experience from doing just that. Witnessing people explore why they think the way they do, why they feel the way they do, why they interact with others the way they do, and how they've come to develop the story they carry is potent and powerful. There are so many moments I will never forget: sitting across from someone in my softly lit office, knowing that the silence means something is shifting within them. Moments of tears as we slowly and gently see patterns more clearly. Moments of joy as they say, "It's such a relief to understand I'm like this for a reason—that it's not because something is wrong with me but because something happened to me." Moments of gratitude as they experience real change in their emotional well-being. These moments are life-altering, and everyone deserves to have access to this type of healing.

Working with other humans up close reminds me of how much we all have in common when we strip away the differences and get to the root. We all want to feel loved. We all want to be heard and seen. We all want to be understood. We all want to belong.

We all want to feel enough, just as we are.

That's what I'm discovering on my healing journey.

I once told myself a story that went like this: I would never be lovable, be accepted, or belong as who I was because my full self wasn't enough.

And I rewrote it. My new story goes like this: I am a person who is innately lovable, who is inherently acceptable, and who deeply belongs to myself and therefore to the world. I am enough, just as I am. Living from this new story (albeit not 100 percent of the time) has completely shifted the way I perceive myself and the ways in which I show up in the world. It has changed my life.

If you have ever felt like you didn't belong, or like you weren't worthy exactly as you are, or like your full self wasn't enough . . . it might be time for you, too, to tell yourself a new story.

This book is about getting honest and exploring how your own stories affect you—and, as you will discover, they probably affect a lot more than you realize. It's about doing the brave work of reframing your stories so you can choose to show up differently for yourself. And it's about getting free by integrating all parts of who you are—the messy and the beautiful—in order to live a truer, more whole, and more meaningful life.

This book is a guide, a companion, and a love letter. It's about learning what tools you can lean on when healing feels hard. It's about holding space for your experiences while also holding space for something new to unfold. It's about offering connection and community—a reminder that you aren't alone, which is something that helped me on my own healing journey.

If I'm totally honest with you, I am *still* in my own process of healing. It hasn't ended, been completed, or come to conclusion. I haven't figured it all out or gotten to the "other side." In the "self-help" world, there's often a message that creates hierarchies between us—that puts certain people on pedestals and names them "experts" or "gurus" or "authorities," as if they somehow have something we don't. I don't believe in hierarchies, and I am not here to share another "I did it and so can you!" story. I'm here to share some of my own truth and what I've gleaned along the way so you, too, can share your own truth. I'm human, right alongside you, and my healing continues to unfold in new ways as I continue uncovering new pieces of myself. I'm writing this book for me, too.

As I shared before, healing ebbs and flows, and even with all the inner work I've done, I continue to explore the stories I'm telling myself. I still have days when I feel like I don't know what I'm doing. I still have moments of total confusion and disconnection. I still experience periods of depression. I still get caught in the wave sometimes. I write, teach, and work from a place of being on the path with you—being on the path of continued healing, being on the path of allowing myself to be fully human first.

The most important thing I've learned about being human first is that I don't have to be ashamed of this fact, and neither do you. We don't have to become perfect to be good. When we give ourselves the opportunity to unlearn the stories that keep us feeling broken and less than, we can relearn our inherent goodness. The goodness that has always been there, underneath what's been piled on top of it, as we've moved through our lives. The goodness we often forget. The goodness we often don't believe or see. The goodness we were born with and will always contain, no matter how much pain we might experience along the way. Because you—we—have always been enough.

Throughout this book, I am going to share with you many of the mindsets and practices that have supported me and others on this healing journey in three parts: Getting Honest, Getting Brave, and Getting Free. Getting honest is about confronting and exploring our beliefs and the stories that grow from them, how they show up in our lives, and what impact they've had on who we are. Understanding the way our stories are woven throughout our lives gives us the awareness we need to move forward with clarity. Getting brave is about doing the courageous work of uprooting the stories holding us back, and creating new ones. This work allows us to decide who we truly are. Getting free is about carrying our new stories forward. It's about embodying what we've discovered through the difficult yet beautiful work outlined here, in a way that supports our full humanity, our goodness, and our inherent enoughness. This work allows us to have a say in how our stories, and our lives, unfold.

Within these parts, I'll share my own journey and those of some composite characters, based on my experiences in working with people. I hope these narratives illustrate just a few of the common ways our stories affect us throughout our lives, as well as what it looks like to reframe those stories and integrate new ones. While we all have different experiences, I believe so many of our stories are also similar. Stories of needing to be perfect to be worthy, of your needs not mattering, of being an imposter, of needing self-criticism to stay in line, and of not belonging are commonly told; they are all based on that root belief of not being enough—they just show up within us in different ways.

I strive to give you not just practices but ways of being, thinking, and showing up, questions that guide you back to your own wisdom, and reminders of all you already contain within you. You are *already* enough. You do not need fixing—you just need to remember who you are underneath the limiting myths you've held about yourself for so many years. Who you are underneath it all is so deeply magnificent.

May this book humanize your healing. May this book honor your process. May this book be less about fixing yourself and more about remembering yourself. May this book make space for the messiness, right alongside the beauty. May this book offer you a refuge from it all. May this book hold you as you rediscover how to hold yourself.

Welcome. I'm so glad you're here.

Ten Loose Guidelines for
Engaging with the Book

1. Our stories are sensitive, personal, and sacred. I encourage you
   to treat yourself with as much compassion and kindness as possible while you work to understand the stories you come from
   and live into. What a gift it is to offer yourself some gentleness
   and grace along the way.

2. While this book will cover a lot, it won't cover everything. It
   might not cover your experience, exactly—you're a unique person with a unique history. And it is not directed toward those
   with severe trauma or other mental health challenges. I want to
   clarify this point so you don't assume something is wrong with
   you if everything in the book doesn't resonate with your unique
   circumstances. I invite you to seek out individualized support if
   you'd like it, whether through therapy or coaching or mentorship (or any other modality I discuss throughout the book!).
   We don't have to go at it alone. We were never meant to.

3. A lot of books might pretend to know exactly what you need in
   order to become a completely, totally, undeniably self-actualized
   human . . . right now. This book won't do that. Quick fixes
   are appealing, but they don't usually sustain. Healing is a long
   game, my friends, and allowing healing to be an ongoing process instead of a destination to reach brings a greater sense of
   acceptance to where we are now. Think of the stories, practices,
   tools, and resources in this book as guides instead of directions.
   I won't be another authority telling you what to do. Instead, I
   hope for this book to be an offering, an idea, a collaboration,

an invitation, and a reminder of all you already hold within yourself to heal, grow, and thrive.

4. This book contains my own experiences, witnessing, learnings, ideas, and insights. Some of them may differ from yours, and this is totally okay. I encourage you to note where you may disagree and allow yourself to explore why. I am not always right.

5. You are your own best healer. My hope is that this book will invite you to tap into your own power as you move through exploring how to carry your story, and yourself, forward.

6. Life ebbs and flows. Some seasons are more difficult, while others feel more easeful. I invite you to keep this in mind as you explore your own story, knowing you don't have to reach a certain place in order to experience some of what I share in this book.

7. Healing is hard sometimes. Don't forget to take breaks, to laugh, to find joy, to seek pleasure, to practice lightheartedness, and to just *be*. As you will learn, these moments and acts are a crucial part of healing, too. We can get so caught up in improvement that we forget we're not actually projects to fix; we're humans.

8. Healing is not another thing at which to project our perfectionism. Perfection isn't possible or required. Not in healing, not in reading a book, not in doing the work described here . . . not in anything. We often want to heal perfectly, grow perfectly, change perfectly, and make sure everyone around us is comfortable and okay with it at the same time. Perhaps letting this process be a little messy is what will support healing. The mess holds its own kind of magic, I think.

9. Don't forget to continue thanking yourself for choosing to show up for yourself in this way, in whatever way unfolds from reading this book, and in every moment you keep going. I see you and I honor you.

10. You can begin again, over and over, forever.

Addressing the Collective Story

One piece I often see missing in the self-help world is a discussion of how the collective story impacts our own. I think of the collective story as the story that plays out in the systems we live in, all of which impact our individual stories. We tend to hold people solely accountable for their own healing without addressing the very real, very valid external factors that contribute to their challenging stories in the first place. I think of people telling a Black woman to "love and light" her way out of micro-aggressions. I think of people urging folks in the LGBTQIA community to meditate their way out of feeling targeted by hate crimes. I think of our culture telling us to rest while also prioritizing and rewarding limitless productivity. I think of our culture insisting that thinking positively will heal those who are living in a world that doesn't create safety for them. It's very easy for me, a privileged white woman with an education, to talk and write about self-care and healing and self-acceptance. What I want to also acknowledge is how much more difficult these things are for folks who are trying to find enough money to put dinner on the table, who are navigating oppression and violence, and who are living in environments that are not at all conducive to anything other than simply surviving another day. Not all of our challenges are for us to fix—they may be for systems to recognize and change.

I share this because the mindsets and practices in this book (or in any book) won't heal everything. Self-compassion won't directly fix racist policies. Mindfulness won't heal centuries of harm toward marginalized folks. Journaling won't heal the wounds of being thought of as less of a human because of who you are. Meditation won't heal inequality. I don't want to pretend like doing the inner work will fix what's happening externally because it won't. This reckoning can be challenging. It can feel like an uphill climb to work on finding ways to show up more fully in the world when the world doesn't always make it safe for everyone to show up fully. It can feel trite to share some of these mindsets and practices; I know, and I've witnessed in my clients, that all the mindsets and practices in the world won't eliminate the very real harm that so many experience daily from external forces.

Individuals regularly feel the burden of "fixing" themselves enough so that they are no longer affected by these external factors. While this might be realistic for some, I find it harmful to put such pressure on the very folks who need systems to change in order to feel safe and secure in this world. As both a professional and a human, I choose to have these hard conversations because the alternative is to continue remaining silent and participating in the problem, rather than addressing it and creating as safe a space as possible (which isn't always possible) for the people who desperately need it.

So before we go further, I want to pause and validate how understandable it is to find so many of these mindsets and practices difficult. I want to honor how hard it is for so many people to keep going in a world that doesn't make them feel wanted. I want to acknowledge how unfair it is that we ask you to do this work in a society that isn't doing the work to make sure you feel valued, safe, and loved. You deserve an environment and space that welcomes you with open arms, that recognizes your inherent importance, that honors your uniqueness, that appreciates your gifts, and that knows your worth despite any and all differences. You matter and your existence matters, and I am so sorry this society doesn't always make that apparent.

While I know that what I share in this book won't heal or fix all the external factors affecting so many of us on a daily basis, I do hope that some of the mindsets and practices will allow you to start seeing ways *you* can show up for yourself, even when the world isn't showing up for you. I hope these offerings will empower you to recognize your internal strength, even when you shouldn't have to continue being strong in the face of everything happening. I hope the exploration of story allows you to separate yourself a bit from the stories being told about you—I hope you recognize your ability to shift the story *you* tell about you, despite any and all outside noise. I hope the words in this book offer a reminder that you're not alone and you can control the way you show up for yourself and in your own life, even when all challenges might not disappear as your own inner stories shift.

As we find ways to heal within, we also need to acknowledge and discuss the ways in which the collective story we are living in is harming so many people. It shouldn't be an individual's job to constantly be trying to heal from the symptoms caused by the collective. We (especially white folks with privilege) must also talk about how we can support ourselves and our neighbors through advocating for policy change. Through voting. Through participating in democracy. Through volunteering, when we have the emotional capacity. Through learning about the history of oppression and discrimination in America. Through acknowledging privilege. Through listening. Through choosing to see people. Through compassion and empathy.

It can feel like an impossible task to keep pushing, keep feeling hopeful, and keep fighting in this place we're in. I, for one, will always make more room for hope than I do for anything else, though. As I frequently tell clients, I will make room for hope for you when you can't do it yourself. I will keep believing things can change, the collective can shift, and we can all find a wider space of healing and shifting the collective story we're navigating in our own ways. I'm deeply grateful to Black, Indigenous, and People of Color, the LGBTQIA community, the body-positive community, and all other communities that are leading the way in teaching us about integrating this work into our lives.

Some people I continue to learn from in relation to the collective story: Tricia Hersey, Rachel Ricketts, adrienne maree brown, Resmaa Menakem, Sonya Renee Taylor, Rachel Cargle, Jennifer Mullan, and my past clinical supervision groups and supervisors.

UNDERSTANDING OUR STORIES

The first place I spoke parts of my story aloud outside of a therapy office was as an undergrad at UC Santa Cruz. I took a moral psychology seminar, and our final project was to write a thirty-minute presentation about some aspect of our lives that we continued to carry within us. I chose to talk about my abandonment, my relentless search for my identity, and my history with depression (you know, the light, casual stuff). I stood in front of my classmates—and on the edge of myself.

"I realize my abandonment had nothing to do with who I am as a person or my worth as a newborn," I said. "That's how it affected me, though, and those are the beliefs that I formed about myself, whether or not they were valid. I have carried these beliefs with me throughout my life."

I explained that these beliefs carved paths for an unhealthy relationship with myself and for challenging relationships with others. "It's not all bad," I said, "and I have made remarkable progress in my life between when I was fourteen and where I am today, but I still have a long way to go."

I said things I had never spoken about with more than a few other people. I shared parts of me that I thought needed to be hidden. Parts I wanted to keep buried. Parts I was still ashamed of. Parts I once wanted no one else to see in me. At the end of the presentation, I read out loud a letter I had written to my birth mother: "My soul longs to meet yours, not only to ask you questions but also to embrace you and tell you that it's okay. It's okay. I know that while I have struggled, you have also struggled. I know that when I think of you every year on my birthday, you may be out there, thinking of me."

I thanked my birth mother. I thanked her for being brave enough to carry me just long enough to let me go. I thanked her for providing me with the opportunity to love, to feel pain, to experience joy, to embrace friends and family, and to discover who I am and what I want from this life. "Without you, I would not be," I said.

I could barely get through the rest of the letter. Tears were at the back of my throat. A swirl of dizziness overcame me.

When I finished, there were a few seconds of silence. I stared at the floor, heart beating fast. When I looked up, most of the people in the room were in tears. My professor put his hand on his heart. They had seen all of me, and they met me with open arms.

I stood, wobbly kneed, in awe of what transpired when I chose to share the hard parts of my story instead of the easy parts—when I chose to finally tell the truth.

I think about that moment often. Writing that letter changed me, and reading it out loud changed me more. It was a potent reminder of what making room for our stories to come out of hiding does: it allows *us* to come out of hiding, too. Understanding my story hasn't fixed or changed what has happened in my life, but it has allowed me to let myself be witnessed as my full self—and to heal. We all deserve this.

Reframing our stories starts with understanding them. It's challenging to have compassion for stories you don't understand, let alone to share them with others, which is why cultivating a deep understanding of our stories first is so transformative. It's why we start here.

Human instinct is to tell stories. In 1944, psychologists Fritz Heider and Marianne Simmel conducted a study in which subjects watched an animated film of shapes moving around a screen, and found that most of the subjects, when asked to explain what had happened, constructed a story about it. This is our way of making meaning of what we experience. It gives us a perceived feeling of control. Creating internal stories can be an unconscious process. We may not even realize what we are telling ourselves until we slow down and start paying attention. That is exactly what this book will support you in doing: tuning in to start understanding your story, gently and tenderly, so you can rewrite the parts that are holding you back and move forward, more whole. Understanding, reframing, and then integrating your story is part of how this healing happens. Getting honest leads to getting brave, and getting brave leads to getting free.

A gentle reminder: You might already be feeling a bit of heaviness about diving into some of your own stories. This is normal. I invite you to go at your own pace, to give yourself permission to pause and to breathe. This is a process and not on a time line. Keep checking in with yourself as you read, and thank yourself for doing this work.

How Our Stories Come to Be

Throughout the book, I will use the word "story" often. You might be wondering, what exactly is a story? I think of our stories in two ways: what we've experienced and what we tell ourselves *about* what we've experienced. Say you're trying a new recipe for a chocolate cake and you leave it in the oven too long—and it burns. The story you've experienced is: I burned the chocolate cake. The story you tell yourself *about* what you've experienced is: I can't even make a chocolate cake.

Our stories are both what
we've experienced, and
what we tell ourselves *about*

what we've experienced.

Our stories can be both small (I can't make this recipe correctly) and big (I'm a failure). Our stories can be both supportive (I tried a new recipe, and I did the best I could) and painful (I can't even make a chocolate cake; I'll never be able to cook anything right). They are not always true, but they get interpreted as true when we repeat them enough. Jill Bolte Taylor, a neuroanatomist, has shared that the lifespan of our emotions is approximately ninety seconds. Isn't that wild? What I infer from this information is that it's the stories we create *about* those emotions that stay with us, not the emotions. The emotions themselves are fleeting—until they become a story.

Without stories, an emotion is just an emotion. A feeling is just a feeling. An experience is just an experience. However, we humans are meaning-making machines. From the beginning of time, humans have been designed to make meaning of what happens in our lives as a form of self-protection. Life can be chaotic, uncertain, and overwhelming—making meaning of everything around and within us is a way to move forward with a perceived sense of safety.

As children, in particular, we desperately want to make sense of the world. Dr. Daniel Siegel, a professor of psychiatry and prominent neuropsychiatrist, has shared about the importance of what he calls the four *s*'s in attachment: Seen, Safe, Soothed, and Secure. Without experiencing these four *s*'s, it becomes easy for children to develop narratives about themselves in response to their needs not getting met. If you grew up in an environment of neglect, disconnection, chaos, uncertainty, or abuse (and this list could go on forever because adverse childhood experiences—an area widely studied by pediatrician and current surgeon general of California, Dr. Nadine Burke Harris—are expansive), you might have developed a story to keep yourself safe.

Examples:

- If your caregivers were often angry, you might have developed a story that you need to stay quiet and small in order to protect yourself from getting hurt.
- If your caregivers were unpredictable in their care for you, you might have learned the story that you aren't deserving of regular care in order to manage your expectations when you didn't receive care.
- If your caregivers physically or emotionally hurt you, you might have learned the story that something is wrong with you in order to make sense of a pain you did nothing to provoke.
- If your caregivers placed more value on what you did than who you were, you might have learned the story that to be good, you had to be perfect and productive in order to be seen by your caregivers.
- If your caregivers were experiencing their own mental health struggles, you might have learned the story that caring for others was more important than caring for yourself in order to normalize the reversal of caretaking roles.

In all these cases, children learned to make sense of their caregivers not knowing how to show up for them by molding themselves into who their caregivers needed them to be. Children learned that if they could just figure out the "right" way to be, maybe they would get the care they needed. You can see how this becomes a difficult burden to carry.

That's the thing about making meaning. It starts off as a resource that supports us. But it gets tricky when the meaning we assign to things isn't accurate. Deb Dana, a lead expert in Polyvagal Theory, often says that "story follows state." By this, she means that our stories often follow our nervous system's responses to the world.

As we grow, what starts as a protective measure results in a story about ourselves that keeps us small, stuck, and disconnected.

Reflection questions to explore your own meaning-making:
- What was your relationship like with your caregivers?
- What messages did you frequently hear growing up?
- How might you have grown in order to make sense of your experiences?
- How did you learn you needed to be a certain way to maintain connection?
- What meaning have you made of what you've been through and learned?

Other Factors That Contribute to Our Stories

Even if you grew up in a relatively "healthy" household, your surrounding environment, culture, and community may have impacted the stories you developed about yourself. Our stories come from many different places, and sometimes the *where* is less important than understanding *how* our stories are showing up in our daily lives.

Family

As children, we are constantly taking in information from our caregivers. This starts before we are even born—our mother's environment, self-talk, support, and experience begin affecting us as early as in utero. Studies show that prenatal stress, mood, and experience all impact the infant and even shape the brain as it develops. For

Some of the factors that shape
our stories included family, trauma,
environment, media, and society.

example, studies indicate that stress hormones during pregnancy can influence the developing baby, which in turn can increase the risk for learning and behavioral challenges for these infants as they grow.

In many ways, our stories can start long before then. We inherit stories that aren't even ours to carry. The study of intergenerational trauma explores how trauma is passed down from generation to generation through stories we inherit, whether we're conscious of it or not. Our family's history impacts who we are. It's in our bodies. Take, for example, the children and grandchildren of Holocaust survivors. According to researchers, the descendants of people who lived through the Holocaust can have lower levels of cortisol, a hormone that helps us respond to stress, than their peers. This trauma changed their biology. The same can be said for other traumatic experiences our ancestors survived and later carried with them.

And once we're born, we note everything we hear and see. We are tiny sponges, absorbing what we experience before we know how to understand clearly. If you witnessed your caregiver constantly criticizing their weight, you might internalize the story that being thin gives you more value. If you heard your caregiver dismissing their own emotions, you might internalize the story that emotions are to be hidden. If you saw your caregiver numb their pain with alcohol or shopping or food, you might internalize the story that hard stuff is to be numbed instead of felt. If you heard your caregiver telling you to "suck it up" or "stop being so sensitive," you may have internalized that sensitivity is weak. When we don't know better, we know what we know—and in childhood, what we know comes from what we see and experience.

Because many of our caregivers were rarely given tools, insights, or education about things like addressing trauma, regulating emotions, and building healthy relationships, they, too, were doing the best they could with what they knew. They didn't have as much access to the information we now have about these themes. We're all imperfect humans interacting with other imperfect humans, and this easily leads to inheriting beliefs and stories that don't always reflect the truth of who we are.

It isn't until we gain some independence that we can see the familial stories we've been living in. Once we do, we can choose to confront the stories we've inherited that we no longer want to participate in. This can feel threatening to our connection with family; it can create fear of being unloved, left out, or even shunned, which is why so many people continue going along with family beliefs, traditions, and stories that don't actually reflect their values or truth.

Trauma

Along with intergenerational trauma, you may have also experienced personal trauma. Bessel van der Kolk, a leading trauma researcher, has shared that trauma is "anything that overwhelms the body's ability to cope." We often think of trauma as big events like a car accident or war, but trauma can also be the result of more repeatedly subtle yet impactful experiences: being emotionally neglected, not experiencing deep connection, having unstable environments or relationships, not getting your needs met, witnessing violence, living as a marginalized person in our society . . . There are many experiences that could qualify as trauma and are much more common than we think.

Awareness of these experiences in our lives can help us understand our stories. It reminds us, again, that when we don't know better, we know what we know. We did our best to make sense of what happened to us from the only information we had at the time.

Environment

I didn't grow up around any adoptees aside from my brother. I remember wondering why I didn't know anyone else who was adopted and what that meant about me. Did it mean I was in the wrong place? Did it mean I was weird? Did it mean something was wrong with me? I asked myself these questions countless times. Not knowing other people who were similar to me made parts of my experience as a child hard; it felt even harder because I blended in. I looked like my family. Everyone assumed that I was just a "normal" kid. Everyone assumed that nothing was wrong. All of this made it really easy to believe that feeling something was wrong was my fault, and that something was wrong *with me.*

I occasionally think about what would have been different if I had been connected to other adoptees, if I'd had the space to explore that part of my identity with people who understood it. Because of my experience of lacking this connection in my environment growing up, I also think about how deeply we are affected by our environment—either what we have in it or what we don't have in it—what we're surrounded by or not surrounded by—what we see or don't see—what we hear or don't hear—what we witness or don't witness. Our environment also impacts what we have access to, what resources are available to us, and how connected we are to community, support, and collective care. Our environment is sort of like a home to the home we carry within us, and so it, too, influences how we relate to ourselves and each other. Exploring the ways in which

Note: this book doesn't necessarily speak directly to trauma and may not be relevant to working through it. Working with a trauma-informed professional and getting individualized support is critical when seeking healing around trauma. There are resources throughout the book that may be helpful to explore in your own life.

your environment shows up in your story holds information about how you've developed into who you are. How has your environment affected you?

Media

Our stories come from childhood, but that's not the *only* place they originate. We are inundated with stories of who we should be and what it means to be "good," "acceptable," "desirable," and "successful" all the time, through all phases of our life.

The wide world of media highlights certain stories, certain bodies, certain lifestyles, certain goals . . . you get the picture. Ideal images are what we reguarly see, and those images seep in and affect the stories we create about ourselves: stories of our body not being thin enough, our relationships not being perfect enough, our goals not being big enough, our home not being styled enough, ourselves not being young enough. The stories we create based off of what we're fed every day can impact us in ways we're not even aware of.

This is especially true today, in the age of social media and the Internet, where it is even easier to access the narratives pushed by our wider culture about what we should strive for. Images of perceived perfection are showcased daily, and comparison runs rampant. Our inner stories are often cultivated from outer expectations, norms, and systems that aren't always designed with our well-being in mind.

When we take in these stories long enough, we start to internalize them. We might even attribute part of our worth to whether or not we're meeting these externally created standards of what we "should" be like and what our lives "should" look like.

Understanding the messages we receive daily and how we might internalize those messages is key to recognizing the stories we carry, and which ones aren't actually ours to carry in the first place.

Society

We don't live in a bubble—we live in a society with stories of its own that get filtered into our lives in various ways. Media is a part of it, but these stories are repeated in all sorts of places, from school curriculums to government ordinances to religious doctrines to any sort of societal norms. Today America is submerged in a culture of capitalism, patriarchy, and white supremacy that values rich over poor, men over women, straight over queer, abled over disabled, thin over fat, and white over Black, and America's stories perpetuate these values. Sonya Renee Taylor, author of *The Body Is Not an Apology*, has taught me so much about how our inner world is impacted by the systems we live in. What stories did you inherit about what it means to be a man or woman, or about what it means to not identify with either gender? What stories did you learn about the color of your skin? What stories did you learn about how much money you had? Your clothing? Your neighborhood?

We are constantly surrounded by stories telling us what we're "supposed" to be like, how we're "supposed" to act, what time line we're "supposed" to be on, and who we're "supposed" to be, based off of cultural norms and standards (that were all made up). What stories did you inherit about what you could and couldn't do with your life—how you should and shouldn't feel about yourself?

Societal stories were perpetuated everywhere when I was growing up. They were also perpetuated everywhere when my parents were growing up, so they quickly became not only societal stories but also familial stories. Our personal stories are shaped by our familial stories, which are shaped by our societal stories. It's natural for us to look inward, but we must also recognize all the ways in which our personal stories are intertwined with the stories that we have inherited and that we have heard.

This is especially important for those who feel like they had a "good" childhood but still carry painful stories about themselves. It's easy to compare pain . . . to assume that because someone has it worse, or someone has a harder story, your pain and story don't count and don't matter. We're taught to view one another in hierarchical ways—to compare ourselves as better or worse, more or less than. The truth is that since each of us has our own unique, individual lives, we also have our own individual pains and stories, right alongside everyone else's. You don't need to prove your pain, your challenges, your harder experiences, or why you hold hard stories within you. You can just honor what's there and let others do the same.

As you can see from the many different places our stories can begin, our whole life is a story. Our beliefs are a story. How we think about ourselves is a story. How we feel about ourselves is a story. When I think about envisioning these different parts of ourselves as stories, I feel a sense of freedom—if stories are made, then stories can change. I hope you, too, feel that as you read. We can recognize the lessons we learned during past chapters and turn a new page. Our life is a story, and as we explore and navigate the way our story affects us, we remind ourselves of the power we inherently hold in how our story can unfold, moving forward.

How Our Stories Show Up in Our Lives

While the stories we carry might start in childhood, they can follow us into all areas of our lives.

Early on in our relationship, a year before I gave the presentation to my psychology seminar, my partner and I were sitting in my car in a 7-Eleven parking lot when we got into an argument. It was dark outside, and I felt dark inside, too. The argument was one of those that was initially about nothing but quickly became something. I turned the radio off and filled the car with empty space and a quiet dullness, as if to echo the emptiness I was feeling inside. He was trying to console me, and I wouldn't have it. "You're just going to leave," I said. "You're going to leave. I don't deserve you. I'm a mistake, and I'm your mistake now, too."

This was something I repeated often. I did everything I could to get him to admit he wanted to leave, because somewhere within me was the story that I wasn't enough for anyone to stay. If my birth mother couldn't stay, why would he?

I kept pushing and pushing, insisting he didn't care and didn't actually want to be with me. Every time he tried to tell me that he would stay, that I deserved him, that I wasn't a mistake—every time he told me a different story—I remember feeling so frustrated. I wanted confirmation of my story so badly, even as it hurt.

Finally, he yelled, "I'm not your birth mother. I'm not leaving!"

I broke.

I felt that phrase so deeply in my bones, yet no one had ever said it out loud, not even me. I carried my story of never-enoughness so deeply in my core that I'd projected it onto every relationship I'd ever had. I think so many of us do this: we form a belief about ourselves and then seek out proof wherever we can. It's self-sabotage at its finest and, as I shared earlier, it isn't our fault. It's all we know at the time.

My defenses lowered in the car with my partner that night. I realized I was sitting with someone who didn't believe my story. Somewhere within me, I knew he might be right, although another part of me didn't want to let go of the story I had been carrying. I didn't know how to live without that story. The very thought of doing so was terrifying.

My partner and I broke up a few weeks later because I wasn't able to stop projecting my story onto our relationship. It was so embedded in me that even the person I loved most couldn't unravel it. But his words stayed with me. I spent the next few years diving deep into the work of continuing to uproot the story that was harming me. In those few years, I began dating someone else, thinking it would save me from actually doing the work within myself. I was so used to using someone else to measure my own worthiness that doing it on my own felt impossible. Soon into that partnership, my patterns again resurfaced—I was playing out the same story, this time with another person. I knew I needed to commit to the work on my own.

It was painful, lonely, and full of challenge. More than that, it was the first opportunity I gave myself to ask how my story was still affecting me, even when I didn't want to admit it was.

Our stories weave themselves into every aspect of our lives. They shape our reactions and our choices. They influence how we treat ourselves and how we relate to other people. Our stories are guiding forces in our experience of being human.

They show up in both subtle and obvious ways. Because I was carrying the story that I wasn't enough, I found it incredibly difficult to trust that people wanted me to be in their lives. Like my partner. Here was evidence that someone didn't just think I was enough— someone thought I was amazing! And that evidence didn't fit the story I kept telling myself over and over.

During the time I was on my own, I remember friends urging me to date, but I wouldn't. Our culture has an idea that relationships will save us, fix us, give us everything we need, and fulfill us. The truth is that unless we do that work internally, a relationship will only mirror the work we haven't yet done within ourselves. I stopped putting my healing into anything outside of me and instead called it inward. To empower myself in this way was scary and uncertain and shaky (who was I to trust myself?), but it's ultimately what allowed me to recognize my own ability to heal myself, for myself.

Two years later, my partner—the one who named my story in the parking lot of 7-Eleven—and I found our way back to each other, but this time I didn't need him to be proof of my unworthiness. I didn't need him to heal me, either. I was healing myself. And he eventually became my husband.

Confirming Our Stories

What we look for, we see. What we believe, we see. When we search for proof of something, whether consciously or unconsciously, we will find it. Shauna Shapiro, a professor of psychology and mindfulness expert, shares that what we practice grows; this applies to our stories, too. The more practice we have in believing and living from them, the more real they feel.

In psychology, there is a phenomenon called "confirmation bias." It describes the experience of finding confirmation for what we believe to be true. Because I felt like I wasn't enough, I constantly looked for proof that I was, indeed, right. It was easy to perceive everything as proof of my own not-enoughness not because I wasn't enough, but because I so deeply believed that story—and when we deeply believe something, we do whatever we can to affirm that belief. Looking for confirmation of our stories is a way of consistently validating the belief that they are true, which makes it really challenging to see things through a different lens. But once you start, you can look for proof of the opposite—and make room for the possibility that the stories we tell ourselves about ourselves are wrong.

Perpetuating Our Stories

When our stories show up often enough, we might find ourselves playing them out over and over. We re-create what's familiar. That's what I did with my partner in the parking lot, and my next partner, too. In a way, acting from the stories we tell ourselves is a form of reenactment: replaying the very stories that hurt us in the first place. This isn't because we're broken or sick but because it's all we know how to do.

Acting from my story of never-enoughness has looked like creating friendships in which my needs weren't as important as theirs, minimizing sharing my voice, and continually dismissing my gifts and strengths. It's hard to admit or find the willingness to be honest about these things. Can you relate?

If you can, maybe hearing Jasmine's story will help you understand your own.

Jasmine initially came to therapy to better understand how to accept herself. Getting to know her was such a joy: I easily saw her goodness, generosity, and sweet nature. She didn't see these things as easily, though. In exploring her story, we eventually understood that she felt like she needed to be helpful all the time and constantly appease others in order to be loved and accepted—in order to be enough as she was. This is tricky, of course, because when we define our sense of self by what we do for others, we essentially forget our power. We allow everyone outside of us to control how we feel about ourselves.

One day Jasmine shared an experience she had while supporting a friend. This friend was in the middle of a devastating breakup. Jasmine was having a hard time herself—she was experiencing a lot of stress related to an upcoming interview for a promotion at work, and she was worried about not being able to financially support

Acting from our stories can look many ways.
Here are a few examples:

- Having a story of your needs not mattering and consistently avoiding meeting your own needs

- Having a story of not belonging and consistently avoiding showing up in the world

- Having a story of not being worthy of love and consistently seeking out relationships that harm you

- Having a story of being incapable and consistently avoiding trying

- Having a story of putting others before yourself and consistently minimizing your own care

- Having a story of the world being unsafe and avoiding risks, new experiences, or vulnerability

herself and her family if it didn't go well. But she went out of her way to offer her friend emotional support, even though she herself was exhausted. Jasmine called in a pizza delivery and researched the perfect Netflix binge, then took a seat on the couch as her friend vented about her relationship struggles. And though Jasmine had her interview the next day, she stayed much later than she intended. She ignored her own needs in order to show up for her friend, even though a part of her knew she didn't have the capacity to do so. She felt like she needed to say yes, always, no matter what.

"How do you feel after you help your friend?" I asked Jasmine.

"It feels good at first, but then I move back to wondering what's wrong with me and questioning why no one shows up for me in the same way."

"It sounds like there might be some resentment there—some wondering why you don't get what you give. Is that right?" I asked.

"Exactly. I do so much for people, and no one seems to want to do the same for me. It makes me feel like they don't like or appreciate me. They reiterate the idea that I'm only worthy if I put everyone else first and ignore my own needs."

"What you just said is so interesting, Jasmine. It sounds like you *know* showing up in this way ends up making you feel unworthy, yet it's how you continue to show up. Do you see how *you* might be the one reiterating your own story of being unworthy unless you're helping others? Can we get curious about that?"

She looked at the plant in the corner of my office—a place she often looked when she was thinking or needing a second to let something sink in a bit deeper. "I'm the one who shows up for people in ways I don't need to and then automatically assume others don't do that for me because I'm not worthy of it. It's like I want to confirm my own story," she said. "I'm the one trying to prove that I'm unworthy."

"The fact that you can see this is incredibly self-aware," I said. "I know it's so challenging to confront these stories. What are you feeling as you share this?"

I always try to slow down the process of unpacking these explorations with my clients. We can easily move too fast and scare ourselves out of going to the hardest places.

"I feel sad," she said. "And relieved." She looked back at me. "I feel like it's starting to make more sense why I go so out of my way for people. That's what I think makes me worthy, so of course that's what my priority is."

"Yes," I said. "And because we can't find our worth outside of ourselves, it always falls short, and you are always left still feeling unworthy. It's not your fault."

Through this exploration, Jasmine and I slowly began to uncover her story of being worthy only when she's giving. We were able to weave her story back to her childhood. Jasmine is the eldest of four kids. Both her parents worked when she was growing up, which meant that she helped take care of her younger brothers and sister. Jasmine quickly learned that the only way she got positive attention was when she ignored her own needs and did what others needed of her. "Good girl," she would hear. She got more confirmation that she needed to be needless in order to feel worthy.

Jasmine was deeply parentified, meaning she was put in roles of taking on more responsibility than a child should assume from an early age. Because of this responsibility, Jasmine grew into the role of a helper quickly. She was rewarded by fitting into her family system in this way. You might imagine how easily this role formed the story Jasmine carried into adulthood—that to be worthy, she needed to be helpful. Of course she formed this story . . . it was birthed from the story of her family, which turned into the story of her.

Jasmine continued to seek out relationships and spaces where she could help. She volunteered for a literacy program, even though she was exhausted from her job. She formed friendships with people who took advantage of her kindness and rarely asked how she was doing. She said yes to tasks at work that were out of her pay grade and not her role, like setting up monthly team meetings and organizing the yearly holiday party. Jasmine's choices perpetuated the belief that she was worthy only when she was helping, so she continued creating situations where her worth was in her helpfulness.

But through digging a little deeper, Jasmine was able to recognize where those beliefs came from and why they made sense. This was the beginning of her writing a new story for herself.

BECOMING AWARE OF
OUR STORIES

We confirm, perpetuate, and live into these harmful stories when we don't have awareness that we're doing so. This is why becoming aware of our stories is both challenging and powerful.

Starting the work of healing old pain isn't easy for any of us. Sometimes we prioritize comfort over change—though change would bring us more fulfillment. Our body craves sameness. Change is uncertain, even threatening; our body wants things to stay the same and alerts us when we try to think, say, or do anything different. For example, when we want to start a new routine, our body might drag. When we want to begin a journaling practice, our body might resist. When we want to practice cultivating a new way of talking to ourselves, our body might automatically turn back to old ways. Our body likes what it's used to. During the process of developing muscles, trying something new feels deeply uncomfortable and even painful. It might feel like you're doing something wrong because of how uncomfortable it is. But with time, the discomfort eases, and our muscles catch up with the work we've been doing. A similar experience happens with our mind. We might be unconsciously pulled back into the stories that hurt us, even if we don't consciously want to be.

I got so comfortable living into a story of never-enoughness that anything else felt impossible. When my partner pointed out that he wasn't my birth mother, I glimpsed what was happening through a new lens for the first time. That tiny glimpse held possibility.

In the hope that I can offer you the same tiny glimpse, I invite you to participate in this guided meditation. Find a seat, take a breath, and tune inward.

As you get comfortable, I invite you to start tuning in to your body in this moment. Is there any tension or tightness, softening or neutrality? Notice that. No need to judge or question—just notice.

As you notice your body in this moment, feel free to breathe into the parts that might feel tense. Send your energy to those parts with tenderness. Allow those parts to soften, if they can. If they can't, notice that, too.

When you feel ready, bring to mind a story you tell yourself often. A story you repeat to yourself when things go wrong, or when challenges arise, or when you're questioning who you are. A story you heard over and over growing up.

Notice what arises within you as you repeat this story. Notice the sensations that get sparked, the emotions that come up, and the feelings associated with the story. Pay attention to the story you tell about the story, the judgments, the criticisms, the hesitation, the questioning, the wanting to run. Notice it all. Let it all be okay.

When do you first remember telling this story? Where? Who did you learn it from?

Who did this story make you feel like you needed to be? How did this story start playing out in your life? What belief is underneath this story?

As you hold the story in your mind, picture it floating by. Picture yourself letting it go. Notice how it feels to witness it leaving your body. To watch it move beyond you. Tune in to what sensations shift or whether none do. Simply notice.

What stories might want to find their way out? What stories are asking to be released? What stories want to be replaced? What comes up when you think about releasing and replacing them?

As you experience what it's like to hold a story and witness it leaving, I encourage you to offer yourself compassion. To recognize the strength it takes to even allow this process to begin. You are so brave. You are so courageous. You are so good.

The Themes That Reveal Our Stories

Often we cannot see the stories we're living out. This is so understandable; it's nearly impossible to witness ourselves while we're in an experience. With perspective, though, as well as with curiosity, we can begin identifying themes—thoughts, beliefs, and behaviors that come up over and over—that might help you become aware of your story. In this section, I've listed some that may have come up in your life. These themes are responses to our beliefs about ourselves. Think of them as outward expressions of the stories we carry.

You might find yourself really resonating with some themes and not so sure about others. I encourage you to take in what feels aligned with your own experiences and to consider the insights. Notice what comes up for you as you continue reading and use the reflection questions as journal prompts, conversation points with a loved one, or simply thoughts to quietly ponder on a walk or with a cup of tea.

Inner Critic: The Voice That Tells You That You'll Never Be Enough

The inner critic. We all have one, it's usually really rude, and it seems to show up when we wish it would go away. The inner critic is the voice inside you that spouts off reasons you aren't enough as you are. It's the voice that reminds you of every single failure you've ever experienced and catalogs all the evidence for why you should just stay small, quiet, and agreeable. As if all this criticism will help us change into a better version of ourselves.

Ironically, our inner critic often shows up when we're seeking growth. It's adept at rearing its head during the moments when we actually need support or encouragement. At work, it might tell us we're lazy or incompetent. In relationships, it might assure us we aren't lovable. In trying new things, it might yell at us not to bother because we'll fail anyway. At every turn, our inner critic seems to have something to say that stops us from showing up in life as our full self.

Our inner critic affects more than how we feel in the moment; it affects our overall well-being. In fact, research has found a strong correlation between negative self-talk (that inner critic) and depression, anxiety, disordered eating, and low self-esteem, among other challenges. This makes sense when you think about it: it's difficult to feel confident and secure when you constantly have someone—yourself—telling you that something is wrong with you. When you aren't aware of your inner critic, that something becomes a fact when in reality it's only a fleeting thought.

My inner critic has, at times, used my story against me. It reminds me that I was abandoned, that I'm not important, and that I'll never measure up. It has caused me to question whether I belong. It wasn't until I realized I had an inner critic that I was able to start using some of the tools I'll share later in this book to separate it from myself, notice it, and tend to it. Now that I'm aware of it, I can see how frequently my inner critic speaks up when I diverge from that old story (by trying new things, sharing my truth, and writing this book). And, I can see that my inner critic isn't me.

If you pause and think about the repeating critical thoughts you have, you might find some commonalities. Are they somehow linked? Do they arise in response to certain triggers? I regularly explore these questions with clients.

Reflection Questions
- What does your inner critic try to convince you of the most?
- When does it tend to show up?
- If it had a name and a face, what would you call it and how would you describe it?
- Does your inner critic remind you of messages you've heard before?
- How does your inner critic hold you back from showing up fully in the world?
- What comes up for you when you think about your inner critic?

It can feel overwhelming when we begin to notice our inner critic, so be gentle with yourself after reading this section.

Perfectionism: The Belief That If You Do Everything Perfectly, You'll Finally Be Enough

Perfectionism is based on the belief that if we just act perfect and look perfect and perform perfectly and achieve perfectly and write perfectly, we'll finally be enough. The challenge with perfectionism is that it isn't even possible, which leaves us constantly grasping for something that will never happen . . . which inevitably makes feeling enough impossible.

Perfectionism takes us out of the present moment and holds us captive in constant striving. It's exhausting. It's painful. And—this warrants repeating—being perfect isn't even possible, which makes it more frustrating.

If you were taught growing up that perfection was expected (some common examples I see include: grades as an indicator of your worth, not getting as much affection if you made a mistake, being forced to take responsibility for your family, or being criticized or belittled), you most likely learned perfectionist habits. What's more, we have all been exposed to a culture of perfectionism that is a result of living in a patriarchal, white-supremacist, capitalistic society. Kenneth Jones and Tema Okun have shared the ways in which perfectionism is a symptom of white supremacy, and viewing it through this lens allows us to see how the systems we live in impact our internal world. In systems that perpetuate continued striving for more, bigger, and better, the pursuit of perfection keeps us out of power. For example, perfectionism is found in the way women are sold an image (often in order to keep buying products). The result of this belief can be seen in shame about natural face blemishes, the belief that cellulite is bad, the idea that we're supposed to look like the "ideal" woman depicted in the media, and more. The ideal of perfection comes from outside us, and we quickly internalize it as a personal problem instead of a systemic issue. In response, you might have created a story that, in order to be lovable, you had to be as close to perfect as possible. I did, even as early on as grade school.

In kindergarten, I was the fastest reader in the class. This distinction was so important to me. Knowing I was adopted, I was terrified that I would be "given back" if I messed up; this fear permeated even my six-year-old self. When another student started reading as fast as I did, my anxiety skyrocketed. I got stomachaches. I was tested for lactose intolerance, but eventually my teacher told my mom that she knew what the real issue was—I was worried. This is how perfectionism started playing out in my own life. Understanding how my story informed these experiences, and all the ones following, was crucial in beginning to heal.

In looking at your own stories and experiences, begin sifting through and seeing how perfectionism has developed in your life. Perfectionism was a way for me to mask my story of never-enoughness. If you have perfectionist tendencies, what story might you be trying to mask?

Reflection Questions
- How has perfectionism shown up in your life?
- Is perfectionism something you've battled with (or continue to experience)?
- Where did your story of having to be perfect come from?
- What have you avoided because you're afraid of doing it imperfectly?
- What thoughts, feelings, or sensations arise when you think about perfectionism?
- In what way does perfectionism impact how you feel about yourself?

Having a Sense of Not Belonging: The Urge to Hide Parts of Yourself in Order to Be Enough

We all seek belonging. And we all *inherently* belong. Simply by being human, we belong. We're all meant to be here, and each of us is connected to one another. I deeply believe belonging isn't earned; it's already in all of us. But many people grow up feeling like they *don't* belong in their own family or community. They might receive messages that they have to conform in order to belong—that belonging is conditional. You might have had parts of yourself shunned by those around you. You might have experienced bullying, criticism, or denial of those parts. This painful experience reinforces the belief that we don't actually belong. When we don't feel safe to be ourselves in one place, the whole world can become an unwelcoming place: it's hard to put ourselves out there, to speak our truth, to be seen for all of who we are.

The consequences can be devastating. We see this everywhere in our culture: in the higher risk of suicide for LGBTQIA individuals, in higher rates of alcoholism in indigenous populations, and in increased rates of depression and anxiety, often coupled with loneliness and isolation. When you feel like you don't belong (and, even worse, are made to feel that way by the wider culture), it can seem impossible to recognize your own value.

For adoptees, feelings of not belonging are common and perpetuated by our culture. And many of my clients come from environments, families, or cultures that pushed a message of not belonging. Because we aren't usually taught how to view our experiences through a different lens, therapy can be the first place clients examine beliefs of not belonging. It is so powerful to provide space for them to explore their belief of not belonging: where it came from, how it developed, and how it holds them back. Helping people do this is critical in guiding them to shift that belief and find the support they need in the places and environments where they *do* belong and always have. This can also lead to profound community building, as seen in support groups or organizations that bring people together through a common shared experience or cause and naturally foster a sense of belonging.

Notice where you question your own belonging. The place that hurts when poked—where there's a wound—is often the place where an old story resides.

Reflection Questions
- Do you question whether or not you belong?
- When did you first feel like you didn't belong?
- What messages did you receive that reinforced this belief?
- Where do you feel you most belong? What environments? What people? What activities? What spaces?
- Does a sense of not belonging impact how you feel about yourself?
- What does belonging mean to you, and how do you know when you *do* belong?

Difficulty in Relationships: The Belief That You Won't Be Enough for Anyone

From the beginning of time, we have been wired for connection. Humans need it not only to survive but to thrive. From the moment we're born, connection is necessary in order for us to grow and learn. We learn how to communicate through connection. We get our needs met through connection. We find safety through connection. We establish a sense of identity through connection. Connection to others is a core component of being alive. The study of attachment echoes this.

When we are cut off from connection at an early age, for whatever reason (abandonment, abuse, neglect, intergenerational trauma, and more), how we act in relationships can change. We might cut ourselves off from our needs in order to become close. Or we might distrust others and refuse to become close. We might hesitate to form friendships or relationships because "everyone ends up leaving." We might sabotage healthy relationships. We might even believe we have to go at it completely and totally alone.

That can lead some to carry certain stories about relationships. If we carry a story that relationships don't end well, we show up from that place. If we carry a story that we aren't deserving of being loved for who we are, we show up from that place. If we carry a story that everyone will leave, we show up from that place. It isn't our fault, but when we aren't aware of our story about what it means to be connected to others, we aren't able to find the meaningful connections we deserve.

My story affected how I showed up with my partner, how much love I allowed myself to receive from him, and how much trust I established with him. Once I became aware of how and why, I was able to begin shifting those dynamics to create healthier ways of connecting.

I see this with clients, watching them play out familial patterns with their partners and friends, or even shut down connection altogether. Once we begin noticing and paying attention to our patterns in relationships, we can start releasing what holds us back from true, genuine connection with others. The patterns that unfold in our relationships can point us back to the stories where those patterns emerged.

Reflection Questions
- Do relationships feel natural for you, or are they difficult to form?
- How are your relationships impacted by the stories you carry?
- What relationships in your past or present have informed your view of yourself?
- What have you learned from your relationships, whether parental, friendships, or romantic relationships?
- Are there patterns you notice in different relationships you have?

People-pleasing: The Urge to Be What Someone Else Wants You to Be in Order to Be Enough

I think of people-pleasing as a pattern of minimizing your own needs for the sake of others, usually out of a desire to be liked. The confusing part is that while it seems to center others, it's actually about ourselves—about feeling like we have to ignore our needs in order to be loved. Putting others first is a way of feeling like we have control of how those people perceive us. When we don't feel good about ourselves, that feedback either makes or breaks us. When we need to make sure everyone else is okay in order for us to feel okay, our whole sense of self gets wrapped up in whether or not others like us. That creates an unbalanced foundation to stand on, let alone grow from.

People-pleasing comes up in all areas of life—even therapy. I have witnessed so many clients hesitating to be fully honest with me (and I've done this with my own practitioners as well). They might skip sharing what's actually happening within them to try to make sure the therapist is comfortable, or to try to manage how they are viewed because they're so used to doing that in their daily lives. When I point out this pattern to clients, their reaction is always interesting, because the recognition tends to feel both embarrassing and affirming—it can feel like being caught in the act of something in addition to finally being truly seen. I have often hidden details or been dishonest about certain feelings or behaviors out of fear that I won't please others. The trouble with this is that we can never feel fully accepted for who we are if we are performing a false version of ourselves for other people.

While people-pleasing might appear manipulative, many haven't learned how to show up any differently in relationships with other people. They may have witnessed their own parents abandoning themselves to please others, or seen people around them curating more appeasing versions of themselves. It isn't our fault that we learn to do this, and with awareness, we can shift it. As we recognize our theme of people-pleasing, we can choose to rely on how we feel about ourselves, rather than relying on how others perceive us, to remember we're enough as we are.

Reflection Questions
- What is your relationship with people-pleasing like?
- Where do you tend to exhibit these behaviors most often? Least often?
- How has people-pleasing made it challenging to show up honestly?

- What messages might you have internalized related to pleasing others before yourself?
- How does people-pleasing affect your daily life and sense of self?
- When you imagine no longer trying to please others as a priority, what arises within you?

Heightened Shame: The Feeling That You'll Never Be Enough, No Matter What

Shame is a result of the deep-seated belief that something is wrong with us; that we are bad. It is even deeper than guilt. Guilt is based on external events—it's about *doing* something wrong. Shame is based on internal beliefs—it's about feeling something is wrong with *you*.

Shame is often internalized from what others say to you or how they treat you. Some examples of how shame shows up: if you felt sad as a child and were told you shouldn't feel that way instead of being supported and heard, you might have internalized that you are wrong to be sad. If you knew you were queer but were told being queer is wrong, you might have internalized that you are wrong to be queer. Shame is at the core of so much of our hurt.

Shame is in constant battle with our worthiness, and it really doesn't like to lose. What's worse is that we are often then given the message to ignore shame completely—to suck it up, to pull ourselves up by the bootstraps, to move on. In some sense, these things can help; in another, they deny us the opportunity to move through our shame.

When we carry shame with us, we also carry the barriers we build to protect others from seeing our shame. But those barriers prevent us from being fully witnessed by others. Keeping ourselves from being truly seen might lead to a tendency to stay quiet and small, or avoid speaking up, or isolate. Shame can result in lack of self-worth, depression, loneliness, and a deep sense of inadequacy. Brené Brown, who has done extensive research on the topic of shame, shares a lot about the implications of shame and how it infiltrates our lives and ourselves.

I have witnessed how pervasive shame can be in others and in myself. It's often the most difficult work clients do in therapy, because it requires going deep into the most hidden parts of the self. Shame indicates that you might be telling yourself a story that something is inherently wrong with you, which is an incredibly painful story to hold. But when we notice the ways shame shows up, we also begin to see a way to reckon with it: we begin to understand our *stories* as being wrong instead of seeing *ourselves* that way.

Reflection Questions
- How does shame show up in your life?
- How does understanding where our stories come from impact how you feel about your own shame?
- What does shame feel like in your body? Physically? Emotionally?
- What messages reinforce your feelings and experiences of shame?
- How do you respond when shame arises within you?
- Growing up, were you made to feel ashamed for who you are?

A gentle reminder: Pause. Take a breath. Notice what you are feeling physically and emotionally. What sensations are there? Where is there tightness? Give those parts of you some extra tenderness in this moment. I invite you to be really gentle with yourself as you think about how these topics show up in your own life. Allowing yourself to do this work and seek deeper understanding of yourself is so brave, courageous, and admirable. You are amazing.

Okay—let's keep going.

Self-doubt: The Feeling That You Can't Possibly Trust Yourself Because You Aren't Enough

Self-doubt is the persistent questioning of our own abilities. It is the hesitation to trust, believe in, and support ourselves. In essence, it is a lack of self-trust. It's hard to trust yourself when you believe that your instincts or judgments are somehow lacking—if you believe you aren't enough.

Often, self-doubt comes from criticism, ridicule, or doubt from other people growing up. If we had an interest in something our caregivers didn't like, we may question if our interests are okay. If we expressed our feelings outwardly when our family didn't show theirs, we might wonder if it's wrong to share our feelings. If we were made fun of for looking a certain way, we might doubt our capacity to trust our own sense of style. When we have different beliefs, values, or opinions than others and there isn't space held for them, we can internalize that experience and start to question the very beliefs, values, and opinions we hold close. Similarly, when our opinions or beliefs aren't heard and acknowledged, we can be led to believe they aren't right, which makes it hard to trust our own intuition.

Self-doubt manifests in a variety of ways. We might find ourselves constantly double-checking before we make a decision. We might let uncertainty stop us from doing something we really want to try. We might question ourselves repeatedly, often to a point of dysfunction. It might even feel hard to stand firmly in our beliefs, or to speak up for ourselves and those around us.

Underneath self-doubt is fear: fear of failure, fear of being perceived negatively, fear of disappointment, fear of making the wrong choice . . . fear of just about anything. The problem is that self-doubt makes it impossible to move with fear, instead of feeling fear and doing something anyway.

Self-doubt often latches on to us when we leave our comfort zones, pulling us back in and thus making it difficult to stretch in new directions. This is why understanding when self-doubt arises is so important: it allows us to see ourselves from a distance, and it may offer us a new perspective on a story that is no longer serving us.

Reflection Questions
- When does self-doubt show up the most in your life?
- How has your story of self-doubt changed over time?
- What parts of yourself do you tend to doubt the most?
- Does self-doubt ever make it hard to trust your choices or take action?
- When you were growing up, what messages did you receive about self-doubt?

Imposter Syndrome: The Feeling That Everyone Will See That You Aren't Enough

Have you ever had the thought *This achievement must be a fluke* or *Everyone else deserves this more than I do*? These thoughts are frequently the result of imposter syndrome (note: it's not actually a "syndrome"—this is just the common terminology). Imposter syndrome arises from the belief that you are somehow tricking everyone into thinking you're worthy when you're not. It also usually includes a persistent worry that you are going to be "exposed" or "revealed" as a fraud. When experiencing imposter syndrome, you feel like the name implies: an imposter.

Imposter syndrome makes it difficult to fully show up wherever we might be—whether in school, at work, or even in relationships. You're always thinking: *I don't deserve to be here!*

Impostor syndrome also makes it hard to value your successes, strengths, and gifts. So we might avoid sharing good news with others, minimize our accomplishments, and question whether or not we're qualified to be doing what we are doing (when the truth is that you are usually more than qualified!). When we experience it often, we essentially hold ourselves back from moving fully toward our dreams, which can amplify its effects.

Becoming aware of when we experience imposter syndrome can be hard, because we may not realize it's something we are carrying until we slow down enough to pay attention and recognize it. This pattern has become quite familiar to me as I've moved through the process of writing this book; luckily, I have awareness of it, so I can separate myself from it a bit more easily than I once did. When we see imposter syndrome as a symptom of our story, we slowly realize that when we know we're enough as we are, we *also* know we deserve to be wherever we are.

Reflection Questions
- Are there any places in your life where you feel like an imposter?
- Where does imposter syndrome show up in your day-to-day life?
- Have you ever been told you didn't deserve to be where you are?
- How does imposter syndrome hold you back?
- When do you most feel its presence, and how do you typically respond?

Now that we've explored some of the ways our stories show up in our daily lives, I invite you to take another deep breath. These topics can be heavy. If it feels difficult, you are not alone; if it feels refreshing or energizing, you are not alone. It's okay to take your time, it's okay to do more research, and it's okay to be not quite sure what to do next. It's also okay if you don't know how any of this relates to you yet.

I encourage you to continue exploring how these themes resonate with you on your own in a way that feels good for you. Do you process by writing? Amazing! Take out your journal and explore what has come up for you through this chapter. Are you a talker? Wonderful! Grab someone you trust and have a conversation regarding what you noticed about yourself through reading this. Are you an artist? Beautiful! Create something that aligns with what came through you in exploring these topics.

There is no wrong way to process, no wrong way to explore, and no wrong way to express—the important part is letting yourself do it.

Here are some prompts to get you started:
- What experiences shaped the way I show up in the world?
- How do the stories I formed about myself affect who I am now?
- What stories am I carrying, and how are they serving or not serving me?
- What stories am I carrying that might not be true?
- Am I carrying stories that aren't actually mine to carry?
- What stories might I want to let go of, shift, or approach differently?
- How is my story influenced by my environment, my ancestors, my family, media, society?
- What themes have I learned because of my story?

As we move into the exploration of how understanding leads to healing, I encourage you to take another breath. Slowly look around the room. Name what you see. Notice how you feel. This is called orienting, and it helps with bringing yourself (and your nervous system) back into the present moment. Thank yourself for being here, for thinking about your own healing, and for doing the work to understand yourself more deeply. It is beautiful and powerful, and I honor you for it. You are so brave.

More Common Stories We Tell Ourselves

I've mentioned several common stories here, but there are countless others we carry in many different ways. Listed below are more examples that might resonate with you.

It's weak to need other people.

It's weak to need help.

Needing other people is a flaw.

I need to figure it all out on my own.

Making mistakes means I am a mistake.

Making mistakes makes me a failure.

Getting it wrong makes me wrong.

I'm supposed to have it all figured out.

I'm broken.

There's something wrong with me.

I can't trust myself.

I need to be liked by everyone.

I have to contort myself to be likable.

I need to hide parts of myself to fit in.

*I won't be accepted if
I show up fully.*

*I don't look like the societal
ideal and therefore I'm ugly.*

*I need to look a certain
way to be desirable.*

*It's unsafe to stand
out and be seen.*

It's safer to stay small.

*I need to minimize myself
in order to be lovable.*

*I need to please everyone
in order to be lovable.*

*I need to be liked by everyone
in order to be lovable.*

I'm unworthy of love.

*No one will love the real
me, so I need to hide.*

*I need to prove why I'm
deserving of love.*

*I need to earn love
and acceptance.*

*It's selfish to center myself
in my own life.*

It's selfish to put myself first.

*It's selfish to take good
care of myself.*

*I have to earn joy, play,
ease, and rest.*

*Productivity dictates
my sense of worth.*

I don't deserve good things.

It isn't safe to have needs.

*I need to be good in order
to get my needs met.*

*I need to be easygoing in
order to get my needs met.*

*I need to act out in order
to get attention.*

I am not enough as I am.

What else would you add to this list? What other stories have circulated in your own life?

Overview of the themes
that reveal our stories:

Inner critic

Perfectionism

A sense of not belonging

Difficulty in relationships

People-pleasing

Heightened shame

Self-doubt

Imposter syndrome

Are there other themes that reveal your
own stories? What are they?

What Function Do Our Stories Still Serve?

You might be thinking about the stories you tell yourself often and wondering, *Why do I keep telling myself this story if it hurts? Why would I create this story in the first place if it's so painful to carry now?*

You aren't the only one who asks these questions. Remember, these stories once served some sort of function for you. They came to be for a reason, and they had a purpose in keeping you safe. I once had a terrifying fear of being given back: I thought my parents would change their mind about adopting me. This fear was wrapped up in my story of never-enoughness. I thought if I talked about my curiosity and yearning to know more about my biological family—if I revealed myself to be anything other than what I imagined a perfect adopted child would be, if I wasn't the fastest reader, and more—my parents wouldn't want me anymore. I kept this longing secret. I thought that if I never talked about that terrifying fear, I could maintain the connection to my parents. I wouldn't disappoint them, let them down, or hurt their feelings. Holding the story of needing to stay quiet about my questions functioned as a safety mechanism, even though it was painful. It wasn't for no reason. This is an example of how we form stories to keep us safe and connected, even if those very stories hurt us at the same time. It wasn't until later, with more perspective and insight, that I realized I could both be honest about my feelings and maintain connection with anyone meant to be in my life—that my feelings wouldn't prevent connection.

Zoom back to younger you. Imagine what you were experiencing, holding, and going through. Bring to life the messages you received, whether explicitly or not, about who you needed to be in order to stay safe. See if you can picture the memories that most deeply affected you growing up, and the beliefs you formed as a result. Ask yourself what those beliefs did for you. Did they protect you? Keep you safe? Maintain connection? Keep you small and quiet (or, conversely, keep you as the center of attention)? Help you feel comforted? Allow you to survive?

Now zoom back further to newborn you. The you who had no clue what was coming. The you along for the ride of whoever carried you, whether or not they stayed. Picture your new fresh skin, your unformed self. Feel the goodness you contained within you from the start. Notice what it feels like to observe even a part of who you've been as good, worthy, and enough. The part that just needed to be yourself. The part that didn't yet know who you were expected to be. Notice how you still carry that part of you within somewhere.

We are incredibly focused on connection. We will do whatever it takes to maintain that connection, including form stories that ultimately harm us in the long run but offer us what we're needing in the moment. Before we formed those stories, we were simply all we didn't yet know. We did our very best with what we had or didn't have. Stories arise for a reason, and that reason isn't a fault of ours.

Because of this, I invite you to thank yourself. Thank the part of you that needed your painful stories to survive. Thank the version of you that clung to your beliefs because you thought you needed them to be okay. Thank the younger you who created these stories, and honor why you might have done so. You have always had your own safety in mind underneath it all, and having compassion for the reason our stories came to be allows us to begin unraveling them.

You Are Not Your Story

Through this exploration, I hope it's becoming clearer that your story is what's wrong, broken, or in need of fixing—not you.

Separating yourself from the story you tell yourself invites a new kind of entry point to self-exploration. It allows for perspective, wiggle room, space to see things differently. It is a way to honor parts of us that we might deny. In narrative therapy, this is called "externalizing"—making *the problem* the problem instead of making *you* the problem. We remove ourselves from the story we've created in order to observe it with more clarity and compassion.

When we consciously separate ourselves from our stories, we create space to respond instead of react, to choose instead of feel like we have no choice, and to determine how we want to approach our stories and ourselves differently. This is incredibly empowering.

It can also lead to beautiful discoveries about our innate worth, underneath the beliefs and stories we've piled on top. How easy is it to notice your faults, flaws, and missteps but completely ignore your goodness? If you're like me, and most humans, it's probably pretty easy. We get so stuck in our stories that we forget about the parts of us that have never fit the harsh narratives we tell ourselves.

My own story of never-enoughness led me to dismiss and even deny parts of myself that went against that story. Dismissal of our enoughness is just another way our stories can show up. Getting compliments felt agonizing because they were in direct opposition to how I felt about myself. It was as if accepting my goodness would be a betrayal to the story I had been carrying about myself.

Separating yourself from your story might look like:

- Giving the story a name

- Talking about the story or problem from someone else's perspective

- Thinking about the story as a visitor instead of a permanent occupant of your life

- No longer labeling yourself as the problem, but instead naming the story as something you are experiencing

I continue working through the stories telling me I don't belong in a book. It would be inauthentic to pretend I've somehow completely overcome the stories I've carried for so long. The beautiful thing is that overcoming it all isn't the point. Never experiencing our harder stories again isn't the point.

The point is to remember everything I've shared here so far. To remember we are more than our hard stories. As I write this book and recognize those stories popping up, I can choose to respond to them differently than I might have in the past. I can choose to show up anyway. I can choose to keep writing, even with doubt. I can choose to keep allowing myself to be seen, even when I question my deservedness of it all. We can all choose in this way.

When I remind myself why these stories might be popping up (safety, familiarity), I can acknowledge those reasons and remind myself that it's safe to show up, that embracing discomfort invites growth, that the unfamiliar holds possibility, and that letting things be different means creating opportunities for my life. What a gift it is to be able to offer that to myself instead of continuing to live out the stories that kept me in fear of being anything different than what I knew for so long. How normal it is for our old stories to arise in seasons of change, on the brink of expansion.

I share this because I want you to know how human it is to grapple with old stories while healing, growing, and shifting. Even for those of us who have been doing inner work for a long time. Even for experts and leaders and people in power. Even for the people you admire most. We are all human here, doing our best to figure it out as we go. Even those who write books about it.

A gentle reminder: You are incredible for exploring these themes within yourself. It takes so much courage to choose to show up for yourself in new ways, which I believe you are doing just by reading this book. I invite you to take a quick moment to honor yourself and the work you are doing. It is not to be taken lightly, and even though we probably haven't met, I am proud of you.

Grieving Our Stories

While sifting through the stories that no longer serve us is imperative in healing, seeking understanding of how our stories came to be can be painful and unsettling. Along with the wide range of emotional experiences that can arise within this process is grief. You may even be feeling a tinge of grief now, which would make so much sense as you explore experiences that might have been painful to revisit and as you've taken a deeper look at your story.

We often don't talk about grief in this way; however, it is present not only when someone dies but when parts of our lives change and end in various ways. Maybe you've experienced this kind of grief before. Perhaps you experienced grief when you moved away from your childhood home, or grew apart from a good friend, or were let go from a job you loved, or experienced a breakup from a partner with whom you imagined spending your life. Coming to terms with your story almost always entails a process of grieving. It might be grieving the relationship you didn't get with your caregivers. It might be grieving what never happened or what you never got to feel. Whatever grief looks like in your own story, acknowledging it is critical. Your grief is valid.

You might not recognize your grief at first. It often comes out as anxiety, agitation, or anger. Those emotional experiences are more familiar, and yet underneath them, grief is waiting to be welcomed. Growing up, I never had conversations about what grieving meant, what it looked like, and how to make space for it in a healthy way.

I couldn't even name this feeling until I was well into my twenties. When I was in graduate school, I continued with a therapist I had seen for years as a late teen. During one of our sessions, I was sharing about this sense of emptiness I was feeling—like there was space waiting to be filled but I didn't know what should fill it. I remember so vividly my therapist asking me if there was a loss that needed to be acknowledged. Immediately, my eyes welled up with tears.

It took me a few moments to parse out what was happening with me, but after a minute or two, I said something along the lines of "There's grief I haven't grieved yet." It had somehow never occurred to me that over the decades prior, I never once acknowledged what I had lost growing up. I had lost a relationship with my biological family. I had lost connection to my ancestry. I had lost a sense of belonging. I hadn't acknowledged it within myself, and no one else acknowledged it for me. Grief was woven into my story, yet I had never named it. And truthfully, grief will always be woven into my story because I will always be adopted—there will always be loss to reckon with in different ways throughout my life. This is why embracing and honoring our grief in ongoing ways is so important and needed.

From what I've witnessed as a therapist, most of us weren't taught how to make space for grief (of all kinds) in our lives. It's another emotional experience we quickly shove down or gloss over. We don't know how to talk about it, so we wonder what it is, why it's there, and why it feels so damn hard. Francis Weller, a psychotherapist and soul activist, shares about grief being *sacred* work, and how necessary this ongoing work is for each of us. He calls it "an apprenticeship with sorrow," this learning of the way grief weaves its way throughout our lives and our being. We must name it. We must hold it in our hands and tend to it with care, as if it is a delicate creature. We must look at it with compassion. When we do this, grief can move. When grief has room, it ebbs and flows.

Until I learned how central grief was to the experience of being human, I didn't know how to honor it. Honoring grief allows me to let go of old stories and welcome new stories.

Letting go of old stories and old versions of ourselves inevitably means loss and, with it, grief. This often feels too scary or overwhelming to confront. As I've shared before, many of us would rather stay stuck than move through the discomfort of change in order to grow and thrive. That's why I believe grief is a key component of allowing ourselves to shift from where we are to where we want to be, over and over again. When we normalize the experience of grief in our lives, and its place in our healing, it becomes less scary and less overwhelming. Grief will always be a deep part of our human experience, so getting acquainted with it is an act of self-honoring.

As you look back at your own life and experiences, I invite you to explore these questions around grief and grieving:
- What did you lose, let go of, or miss that you might not have recognized as a loss?
- What does grief typically feel like in your body—where do you hold it most?
- How was grief talked about and dealt with in your family or caregiving environment?
- How have you allowed yourself to grieve (or not grieve) in the past?
- Where does grief show up the most for you when you reflect on it?
- How have you processed or acknowledged grief in the past?
- Where might you be holding on to unfelt grief?
- What parts of your life might need to be honored through the experience of grief?

- How might allowing grief also allow something new to be created and experienced?

As you explore these questions, specific memories or experiences might pop up. I encourage you to be kind to yourself in this exploration, as grief can be a heavy topic to dive into. Honoring grief as a normal part of being human is a beautiful way to give ourselves permission to allow it, to learn from it, to grow through it.

Validating Our Stories

Becoming aware of our stories leads to grief, but it also leads to validation. Validation is the process of recognizing and accepting something within ourselves or others—affirming our experiences—honoring what we're carrying—holding space for our lived experience. It's what I felt when I shared the letter I wrote to my birth mother with my class at UC Santa Cruz. It's what I've felt sitting on the couches of therapists and in the presence of loved ones. It's what I've felt any time someone has truly witnessed me.

It's what we feel when we remember we're not alone.

I recall being a teenager and sitting on my therapist's couch. She said, "If you feel comfortable, tell me about your origin story."

I told her I was left and didn't know who my birth parents were. I told her I had never talked to another adoptee before. I told her about the time an elementary school teacher insisted I leave my birth parents off of my family tree because they "weren't my family." I told her about how often I was urged to be grateful, how often I was called a miracle, and how painful it was to hear those things but not have my pain validated. I assumed she would urge me to be grateful, too.

But my therapist paused for a few moments and finally said, "Of course you feel this way. Of course. There's so much pain there. Understandable pain. It is not normal to lose your biological family, even from birth." In that moment, my shoulders dropped. My heartbeat changed. My eyes welled up with tears that seemed to have been looking for a way out for years. I felt a sense of relief, even though nothing had really changed—my story was the same, but it suddenly felt a little lighter. Someone could hold all the parts of it with me. I didn't feel so alone. This is the power of validation.

Sharing a piece of the story I was carrying and having it held with compassion modeled for me that maybe I could hold it that way myself. Maybe there was another way. I couldn't change what had happened or how I'd carried my story in the past. I could shift the way I carried my story going forward. I could shift the way I talked to myself. I could shift a lot, in fact, and that moment in my therapist's office was the first time I recognized it.

My therapist offered validation, and that made all the difference. Validation is a reminder that nothing is wrong with us. It's a reminder that we don't need to feel bad for being who we are or experiencing what we've experienced. It's a reminder that we're only human.

Validation is simple, and it's one of the most profound experiences we can have in life. It's one of the things I love the most about reading—seeing myself in someone else's words and realizing I'm not alone.

Can you think of a time when you felt validated for exactly what you were feeling or experiencing? Can you feel in your body the difference between being understood and being asked to minimize, change, or fix how you feel for someone else's benefit? They are very

Validation might look like:

- Being heard, seen, and understood fully

- Having your feelings acknowledged

- Being witnessed without trying to be changed

- Honoring your lived experience

- Listening to understand, not to respond

- Your full humanity being accepted

- Making room for your feelings and emotions

- Holding your story with curiosity, not judgment

- Leading with empathy and positive regard

different sensations—one is freeing, and one is diminishing. One makes room for all parts of who we are and one asks us to hide parts of us. Being validated, both by others and by ourselves, is a way of reminding ourselves we're okay just as we are.

So many of us haven't received validation. We haven't had our difficulties held with tenderness. This isn't because we haven't deserved it but because most of us were not taught how to do that for other people. Our parents might not have had that experience. Their parents might not have, either. We can't replicate what we haven't seen.

In a therapy model called accelerated experiential dynamic psychotherapy (AEDP), a form of psychotherapy that focuses on processing emotion, one of the main goals is to "undo aloneness." This idea is captivating to me because it simplifies so much what therapeutic work is about and so much of what has supported me in my own healing journey: not feeling alone. Undoing aloneness is critical. When we form connections with those who reflect our full self, it's like we stop looking at a tarnished mirror and finally see what's actually there—what's been there all along but has been clouded from us.

I have experienced this as both the one being reflected and the one doing the reflecting. Once I was sitting with a client as she shared a piece of her past that she hadn't shared before. After she talked for about ten minutes about different aspects of herself that she kept hidden, I asked her what it was like to share them. She expressed embarrassment and nervousness but also said she felt safe enough to share those parts of her. I echoed what I saw in her sharing: resilience, overcoming, strength, fortitude, and awe. I echoed what wasn't echoed to her when she had shared those parts of her with other people. I offered validation.

When I did, I noticed her entire body shift. Her eyes softened. Her posture became less crouched. There was a relaxing—an ease.

She began to take in the new reflection I offered. She was embracing a different way of seeing herself. It didn't mean she was suddenly "better." What it did mean (or what it appeared to mean, at least) is that she felt less alone.

These moments can feel wildly meaningful because they're a reflection of what we already know to be true somewhere within us. We just needed to see it and hear it somewhere—we needed the part of us that knows it to be true to be heard and seen. These reflections serve as a reminder of who we actually are, and they can lead us to create new, more accurate, and more supportive stories.

Contemplating Our Stories

No one told me what my story was; I figured it out after years of contemplation, exploration, and diving deep. I allowed myself to get curious and pay attention to the meaning I've made from my experiences and the ways in which my sense of self has been affected by it.

It isn't often prescribed in our culture, but I am, in a way, prescribing it now: contemplation—without the distraction of what others are doing or thinking or feeling—is an incredible healing practice. Contemplation allows us to start forming a relationship with ourselves based on what's happening for us. It also gives us the power to explore our inner world without needing to seek answers outside of us.

Throughout this section of the book, I have shared a *lot* of questions. This is because I cannot tell you what your unique story is. I can't tell you why your unique story has been created or where it came from. No one could make sense of my story for me—only I could do that. I cannot make sense of your story for you—only you can do that. What I can do is offer questions. Your answers will guide you.

We are all unique, complex beings who require different things. As much as we want a direct map, there just isn't a universal one. We are each approaching healing and personal growth from different places, with different kinds of support, with different histories and experiences and personalities and strengths. To say there is one right way for all of us would deny our inherent individuality. Instead, making time for you to contemplate —to have the space and intention to get to know your inner landscape—to have the reminder that you're not alone in doing so—are what I have found to be so transformative in my life and my practice. We forget that we hold the map to our own healing, growth, and change. We have what we need within us.

Next are some further questions to ponder when thinking about your own stories. As you explore them, listen to your inner voice, but seek out support. Use your network. Talk about it in your therapy session. Muse on it as you engage in things you love, whether movement or art or music or whatever your thing may be. The key isn't to figure it all out right away but to allow space to tune inward and explore what arises. You might surprise yourself.

I encourage you to contemplate. To really think about what arrives within you as you do. To notice what comes up first and to ask yourself if that's your response, or if it's just what you've learned to respond with. What answer is underneath the answer?

Questions for Contemplation
• What stories am I frequently telling myself?
• What is my default when something challenging happens?
• How do I typically respond when things don't go my way?

- What sorts of judgment or criticism do I hold toward others and myself?
- What do I find myself repeating to myself at various points?
- Where might I have learned or formed these stories?
- Where have I witnessed or heard these stories before?
- Are any of those stories familiar or recognizable?
- When do I remember first telling myself and believing these stories?
- Did I learn them from my home or environment growing up?
- Did I model them from caregivers or siblings?
- How are these stories impacting the way I'm showing up in my life?
- Where do these stories come up the most? With whom?
- How do these stories hold me back or stop me from living authentically?
- What have these stories caused me to believe about myself or others?
- How do these stories show up in my relationships?
- What stories did others ascribe to me that I have internalized as my own?
- What was I often told as a child that I've inherited as truth?
- How was I treated when I was feeling a lot/having a hard time?
- Was I celebrated in my success and supported in my growth?
- What do I remember hearing often from my caregivers?
- What roles did I fill in order to maintain connection?
- What traits was I often named/called/told I was?
- How have these stories protected me at some point?
- In what ways have my stories helped me survive/stay connected/stay safe?
- How have my stories helped me keep something I needed?

- What did holding on to these stories tightly do for me at different times?
- Why might I have formed these stories or held on to them?
- How did these stories serve me in some way?
- What patterns do I notice now around these stories?
- How often do I notice myself living from these stories?
- What does it feel like when I take notice of these stories?
- What judgments, criticisms, or opinions arise when I notice these stories?
- Do these stories get stronger around certain people, spaces, or environments?
- How do I respond when my stories are present?
- How do these stories no longer serve me?
- What stories have I been carrying that I want to let go of?
- What stories did I need before that I no longer need?
- What stories don't feel supportive for who I am now?
- What stories limit who I feel capable of becoming?
- What stories do I still believe that might not actually be true?
- What would it be like to live without these stories?
- How would it feel to respond with intention rather than from pattern?
- What would change if my stories changed?
- Who would I be without these stories?
- What would feel different if the stories I told myself were different?
- With different stories, how would I show up in my life?
- What stories do I want to make room for, grow, or bring to life?
- What stories feel supportive, nourishing, and accurate?
- What kind of stories do I want to lean on during both joy and challenge?

- What stories would allow my best and most authentic self to come to the surface?
- What stories do I see in those I admire carrying, and how can I find them within myself?
- What stories would allow me to live the kind of life I strive to live?

As you read through and contemplate the stories that continue to show up most in your life, I encourage you to keep note.

- Some of the common stories I tell myself:
- Where I remember first learning/taking on those stories:
- Where they most show up now:
- Feelings I get when they show up:
- How those stories impact different areas of my life:
- People/spaces that reinforce those stories:
- People/spaces that remind me they're just stories:
- Feelings I get when I remind myself they're just stories:
- New, supportive stories I want to write for myself/my life:

Changing Our Stories Changes Our Life

Through becoming aware of our stories, we give ourselves the opportunity to choose how to move forward—and I believe that's one of the most important parts of a healing journey. Choice brings empowerment, hope; it is a reminder of what we have a say in. Exercising our choice in our healing is often a challenging process. Many times the very things that harmed us in life involved *not* having choice. To unlearn those beliefs takes so much courage. Life rewards our courage, our choice to show up for ourselves, and our movement toward healing—though it might not happen in the exact way we want it to or on the exact time line we hope it does.

In my mid-twenties, after I'd wondered for years about my biological family, someone gave me an Ancestry.com DNA kit as a gift. I had always been too afraid to consider taking that step for myself; now I finally held in my hands a potential opening to information I had sought for my entire life but never thought was possible to find. I spat into the little tube and sent it off to be tested. When the results came back, I found out I was Scottish, English, Irish, and Swedish. I could finally identify where I came from in a small but meaningful way.

Below the DNA results were connections—people who matched DNA with me. I was connected to fourth cousins and more distant relatives. I desperately messaged several of them in case they might have somehow known something about why I was left, but I got nothing back. I didn't log back on to Ancestry.com for months.

Until one day when, for some reason, I decided to log on to delete my account. I hadn't used it in a long time, and I didn't want to pay for it anymore. I typed in my password and got an alert: I had a match with an immediate family member. My heart skipped a beat (or five).

I got matched to what I soon found out was my biological sister. Through emailing back and forth, I discovered we had another brother and half sister out there. My sister had both our birth parents' contact information, so I sent my birth mother an email with the letter I had read in front of my psychology seminar years ago, never thinking I'd actually be able to share it with her. She replied. What I had dreamed about since I was a child was now right in front of me. And because of the healing work I had done, I finally felt deserving of and ready for it.

None of this would have happened if I hadn't had the courage to take that test when I took it. It wouldn't have happened if I hadn't thought to log on and delete my account. It wouldn't have happened if I hadn't been willing to confront my story, knowing there was no guarantee of the outcome but choosing to explore it anyway.

It reminded me that trusting the timing of my healing was everything. It reminded me that we can't always rush or move through our healing (what would we miss if we did?). It reminded me that maybe all my questioning and pain and challenge hadn't been for nothing. Maybe a part of me needed it in order to find within the courage to search for what was missing. Maybe I needed to sift through the stagnancy, the pain, the loneliness, and the grief in order to grow the willingness to live into something new—a story that makes more room for what's true—a story of being enough, being worthy, and belonging. All of my siblings attended my wedding to my partner.

Through this experience and to this day, I've understood that even believing there is more possible for us allows more to be possible.

I don't believe any of us should have to face so much of what we do face in our lives. I do, however, believe that when we utilize those experiences for the betterment of our lives and possibly the lives of others, those experiences can become more than just a hard story. They become more when we allow ourselves to stop being defined by them—when we remember who we are without them. Putting down hard stories—stories that diminish our gifts, bypass our goodness, deny our lovability, and keep us feeling less than—changes what is possible; in many ways, it changes our life.

That's what happened with my client Jen. Jen's life looked incredible from the outside. She was pulling straight A's in school, working toward her longtime goal of becoming a nurse. She seemed to reach every achievement she set her eyes on. Her Instagram feed was full of beautiful photos from beach days and barbecues with her close group of friends. Others wondered how the hell she had it so together, and envied her seemingly flawless life. She was the picture of what we perceive as perfection.

What didn't show on the outside was Jen's paralyzing belief that she wasn't good enough. What looked like perfection was actually the result of an exhausting and never-ending pursuit to hide the fact that Jen didn't like herself. She loved her friends but always felt like they were better than she was. She enjoyed school but always felt like she was behind, no matter how well she did. She loved ice cream but had stopped eating it out of fear that it would cause her to gain weight, which she internalized as a negative. She found great joy in dancing but never did it in front of anyone because she didn't want to look silly or mess up. She allowed others to see the parts of her she felt were enough, and hid everything else. The thing is, even when others praised her and admired her—even when she lost weight—even when she got 99 percent on a paper—even when she gave herself permission to dance in her bedroom—she still didn't like herself. She never let her true, messy full self be seen. Perfection became her trying-to-feel-worthy device of choice—a mask for her pain.

When Jen started therapy, she didn't understand what was wrong. She, too, felt like she should have it all together—like she should just be happy, because look at everything going right! She tried to uphold her mask even on the therapy couch because it had become a habit. She'd ask if she was doing therapy right—if she was allowed to talk about certain things—if she was able to choose what we discussed in session. She apologized for taking up space, for yawning, for crying, for being human.

During one session, I asked Jen about this. "I wonder if therapy might be another thing you are trying to do perfectly. I wonder what it would be like to let yourself be messy here . . . to let yourself be honest. And I wonder what stories are arising within you that make it hard to do so. What comes up for you as I share this?"

Jen looked down, hands crossed, as if trying her hardest to contain herself. She started to cry. I told her, "It's okay to cry here, Jen. It's okay." We sat in silence for a few moments as she slowly allowed herself to be with the truth she was holding, and to be witnessed in it. Her imperfection was revealing itself, and I was holding all of it with reverence.

Jen grew up in an environment where mistakes were bad and accomplishments were good . . . where growing edges were judged and achievements were noticed . . . where messiness wasn't allowed, and the more put-together versions of herself were more widely accepted. There wasn't much room to become who she truly was in an environment where anything other than a mask was judged; the rest of her was pushed down or, at worst, ignored.

Jen created a story of needing to be perfect in order to feel good enough in her family. Jen's parents were very successful careerwise but offered very little emotional support. They praised Jen for her external achievements but didn't take the time to get to truly know her. This led Jen to believe that creating an external view of perfection was the only way to be seen as worthy. Jen spent all her time striving, had deep anxiety around getting things wrong or falling behind, and worried endlessly about messing something up.

Jen was tired of striving. She was tired of living from this story and was ready for something different.

Continuing to Unfold

The poet and philosopher David Whyte has a poem called "Start Close In." Part of it says, "Start close in, don't take the second step or the third, start with the first thing close in, the step you don't want to take." I think of this poem often when I'm considering where to begin a journey, a next step, or an inner exploration. "Start Close In" is about starting within ourselves—not jumping ahead out of the discomfort, but turning inward: confronting the truth, looking directly at what's there, and exploring what you find. In the case of our stories, you've already Started Close In: you've begun the quest for understanding, which inevitably creates an opening to something new—something different.

The next section of this book will share some of the mindsets and practices that have supported my clients and me and that I hope will support you as you begin the process of reframing your own hard stories and creating more supportive ones. Taking forward the understanding you've gleaned in this section will allow you to have compassion for the parts of yourself that might find it difficult to shift those stories. It's understandable if it feels difficult, because it *is*! But I have found this process more rewarding than the challenge of staying stuck in my old story. I hope you find this to be true, too.

I invite you to pause before moving on to the next section of the book. Notice what it feels like in your body to confront the stories you've been carrying. Notice what arises within you as you explore your own story and the impact it has had on your life. Notice what might have shifted or changed as you've read about more deeply understanding your story. Notice any feelings, thoughts, judgments, or patterns that come up for you. Notice what is present in you in this moment. No judgment . . . just noticing.

Pausing to pay attention to what we are experiencing is a practice of awareness that allows us to integrate into everyday life what we've learned. We often skip this part—we skip the intentional practice of being with what we've consumed. Later in the book, you'll learn more about why this is so important and how it supports our healing journey.

As you do, I encourage you to reflect not only on all the inner exploration you've done thus far but also on the choice you've made to dive into this work. It is not at all easy to examine your stories from new perspectives. Doing inner work requires a lot from us. I want to honor you for showing up for yourself in this way and for choosing to navigate the stories you've been carrying. It takes so much courage to do so.

I invite you to keep reminding yourself why you're reading this book, why you want to explore the stories you're carrying, and why exploring your stories matters to you. Remembering our why keeps us going when it feels hard. You're doing so, so great.

PART TWO

GETTING BRAVE

REFRAMING OUR STORIES

You are hurting, and I am listening.

I wrote this in my journal a long time ago. It was a time when I was first learning to pay attention to my story. Since then, I've held close this idea of turning inward, recognizing what I am feeling, and choosing to listen. I believe that listening to the stories we've been telling ourselves, as I've described in the first part of this book, is a key step in beginning to make room for new ones.

At this point, you might have a deeper understanding of your story. It might make sense to you why you're carrying it and where it came from. You might be able to identify ways in which your story shows up in your life, how it affects you, and what ways it holds you back. All of this is so amazing, incredible, and worthy of being celebrated (what can you do to celebrate yourself today?).

I want to invite you to pause here. Diving into our stories, our histories, and our experiences can be an incredibly challenging and intense process. Your courage is inspiring and admirable and deserving of your own gratitude.

Here are a few affirmations you can read to yourself, jot down in your journal, or think about quietly as you engage with this inner work:

- I am brave for digging into my story.
- I am courageous for uprooting what I might have been keeping hidden.
- I am admirable for being willing to free myself from my story.
- I am strong for allowing myself to recognize the ways I've been talking to myself.

- I am human for struggling, and I am incredible for making space for my fullness.
- I am enough, even when old stories try to convince me otherwise.

Repeating affirmations to ourselves while we go through any sort of inner work can be so helpful, even when it feels what many would call "woo-woo" (it's not). I share this reminder to pause because doing so in our daily lives, whether or not we're engaging in inner work, is valuable. Creating a habit of slowing down to honor all you've already overcome, worked through, and grown from reminds you of your own resiliency and strength—things we often forget to acknowledge or even recognize within ourselves.

Okay—let's talk about getting brave enough to reframe our stories. Understanding our story leads to *doing something with it.*

In this part of the book, we explore what moving out of old stories and into new ones can look like, drawing on various mindsets and practices. While our stories may be different and our healing process may be different, this part of healing leads each of us to a place that allows us to shift into the truth of who we are and away from the myths we've been carrying. Reframing your story helps you move from what keeps you small to what sets you free.

I've listed many of the stories we carry—we're all unique and different—but I believe they are variations on the same idea. It's my hope that we can all shift our story from *I am not enough* → *I am enough exactly as I am.*

Moving through the discomfort of releasing old stories and living into new ones is a process, but one all of us are deserving of. It is my hope that, through this section, you'll witness what it could look like to untangle from what no longer serves you in order to make space for the worthiness, goodness, and enoughness of you.

From This: → To This:

I need to be perfect → I'm lovable in all my
to be loved   imperfections

I can't → My needs
have needs   matter

It isn't safe to → I can embrace my
be myself   full self entirely

I'm behind → I'm where
in life   I need to be

Something is → Nothing is wrong
wrong with me   with me

I'm broken → I'm just in pain

THE FIVE BASIC NEEDS

TENDING TO YOUR BASIC NEEDS

One of the first things I explore with clients (and with myself) is basic needs. It's easy to overlook the simple, yet the simple is imperative in order to dive into the not so simple. During the process of uncovering, uprooting, unraveling, and reframing the stories we tell ourselves, tending to our basic needs is nonnegotiable.

Because we can easily get carried away in the big stuff, the big shifts, and the big work, we forget how transformative and important it is to tend to the simple stuff. What simple stuff? you might ask.

1. Eating enough food and eating nourishing food
2. Drinking plenty of water and staying hydrated
3. Getting enough sleep and rest
4. Moving your body
5. Nurturing connections and staying involved in community

I think of these factors as the most important in taking care of myself daily. If I'm in a bad mood, I always check in with these five things: have I done them today? If not, I make a plan to do them. It (almost) always helps.

These are ground-level ways of nourishing ourselves that we can always fall back on when everything else feels too hard or too much. Caring for ourselves is often difficult when we don't think we're good enough to receive this kind of care. By engaging in these self-care practices, we are essentially supporting ourselves in shifting into new stories. We are committing to the belief that we are deserving of care. This will, in turn, remind us how deserving we are of care.

Exploring Your Five Basic Needs

To tune in to where you're at and where you might want to create shifts in your self-care practices, here are some questions to explore and come back to often.

1. Eating enough food and eating nourishing food
   What are you eating throughout the day, and are you eating enough? Is the food you eat nourishing you and making you feel satisfied? Do you eat foods that allow your body to feel its best? Are you eating breakfast (and enough to energize you through the morning)? Are you eating foods that bring you comfort and joy, too? (I am not a nutritionist, so if you need more information about food and eating, please consult with one!)
2. Drinking plenty of water and staying hydrated
   Are you drinking water throughout the day? Do you stay hydrated? If not, what might you need to do just that? We forget how important water is for our well-being. We are 90 percent water, so we need a lot of it!
3. Getting enough sleep and rest
   How much sleep do you typically need to feel rested? Are you getting that much sleep? If not, what are the barriers, and what can be changed to prioritize your sleep and rest?
4. Moving your body
   Are you moving your body each day in whatever way feels accessible to you? Do you stretch and nourish your physical vessel? Do you tend to your physical health not in a punishing way but in a self-compassionate way? If not, what might you need to shift it?
5. Nurturing connections and staying involved in community
   Are you regularly connecting with the people in your life? Do

Five Basic Needs:

1. Eating food (and enough of it)

2. Staying hydrated

3. Getting enough sleep and rest

4. Moving your body

5. Nurturing connections

you feel supported? Are you making time for connection? If not, what might you need in order to cultivate connection?

We are much more likely to practice what supports us emotionally if we feel good physically, which is why tending to our basic needs must be at the top of our priority list. Create a checklist, or some sort of reminder somewhere you pay attention, to offer yourself a little boost of support to continue the simple practices that keep you feeling as well as you can.

Two Questions to Ask Before You Begin

While we need many different things as we reframe our stories, as we unlearn, grow, and heal, I think there are two important and integral conditions that allow us to begin the process. I think of these as the foundation of healing—what's needed before you start to build. As with a house, a good foundation keeps everything from tumbling. These conditions keep us supported as we shift from old stories into new ones. They are:

Safety: having a safe space, both within ourselves and with others, to explore, reframe, and integrate our story
Willingness: having a willingness to embrace a new, more supportive story

So, before moving on, ask yourself: What do safety and willingness look like for me? How do I know when I am safe and when I am willing? How can I stay rooted to these conditions in order to create a greater capacity for healing?

Safety

My husband and I recently went on a hike near Oakland. We began up a new tree-covered path, fog rolling in over the hills surrounding us, morning light beaming in through the greenery. I was certain this path would connect us to the main trail . . . eventually. After we walked up and up and up for about a mile, we ended up at the top, and all we found was a dead end and an abandoned energy plant.

My heart started racing, and I felt myself begin to panic. I thought: *We walked all that way for nothing! We're going to be too tired to hike in the good parts now! I can't believe I got us lost!* Stories based out of shame started running through my mind, quietly yet noticeably; more specifically, a story that I couldn't get anything right, further proving my root belief of not being enough. It sounds dramatic as I write, but when we're right in the middle of our stories, these thoughts feel so deeply true.

I decided to stop them right there, after just a few seconds. I took a deep breath.

I named the story I was feeling out loud ("I'm telling myself I can't do anything right and that it's proof I'm not enough").

I spoke a more accurate one ("I got lost . . . just like everyone does sometimes. Everything is okay. I'm okay").

Instantly, I felt relieved. I started laughing at just how tense a simple error made me feel. My partner and I made our way down the hill and found ourselves back at the starting point. We started again, and the actual trail ended up being much more beautiful and lush than the first.

Years ago, that moment would have led me to a full-on meltdown, a parade of self-criticism, a red-flushed face of shame, and a decision to just go home because why even bother now? Back then I didn't feel safe enough to do something different. But that day I felt safe enough to recognize the story I was telling myself and shift it.

We can't do much of anything if we feel unsafe, because if there's any sense of danger, our nervous system and body will respond in certain ways that keep us out of action. Some of the responses include fight, flight, freeze, and fawn, all of which are activated in order to protect us. If you've experienced trauma, these responses might become activated more often or maintain themselves in more long-term ways. (There are so many people who explore these responses in depth, including Bessel van der Kolk, Deb Dana, Peter Levine, Janina Fisher, Pat Ogden, and others, and I highly recommend reading their work to learn more, if this is something you've come up against.) Safety is our innate goal always—we do whatever we need to do in order to keep ourselves safe—in fact, as I shared earlier, feeling unsafe is often why certain stories formed in the first place: as a way of protecting ourselves, keeping us in connection, and maintaining a sense of security.

There are three aspects to maintaining safety. First, internal safety. This includes a regulated nervous system, so you're not in fight/flight/freeze/fawn mode. It means recognizing when we're moving out of our "window of tolerance," a term coined by professor of psychiatry Dan Siegel that describes our optimal zone of arousal (not too activated and not too shut down), and knowing we have the tools to move back into neutral when we do. It also includes external safety, which begins with being in a safe environment. It means knowing where we can go if something happens. Finally, it includes relational safety. We need people we can depend on, who support us, connect with us, and hold space for us. Noting these three aspects of safety for your own life is an empowering practice and serves as a reminder of the ways you can support yourself or receive support. That day on the hike, I felt an internal sense of safety by utilizing tools to bring myself back to my window of tolerance. I took a deep breath. I felt an external sense of safety by noting my surroundings and seeing there was nothing that could harm me. And I felt a relational sense of safety. My husband was right there to remind me I was okay. Experiencing safety allowed me to more easily move through the story I was telling myself and create a new one.

What might safety look like in exploring your story?
- Making sure your basic needs are met and tended to daily
- Keeping your nervous system as steady as you're able to and trusting yourself to move back to center when dysregulation happens
- Having mindsets and practices (breath, movement, grounding, connection, ritual, slowing down, getting oriented to your environment, mindfulness, self-touch, et cetera) to bring you back to your window of tolerance
- Feeling seen and heard by the people you explore your stories with
- Trusting others to hold your story with compassion and acceptance
- Recognizing what safety does and doesn't feel like
- Knowing you can handle what comes up for you in exploring your story, and knowing there is something beyond what you've known up until this point

As you explore what safety might look and feel like for you, I encourage you to make a list of people you feel safe being your full self with. Who sees all of you and still shows up with compassion? Who can you share your darkest parts with? Who loves you regardless of what you do or how you show up?

Ask these questions, too: Where do you feel most safe? When do you feel most safe? How do you know you're safe? What does safety feel like in your body? Getting to know your relationship to safety and your understanding of what it might feel like is an ongoing practice, and one that requires our compassionate commitment.

If you need more support in exploring what safety looks like to you, there are specific types of therapy that you might consider exploring:

- Somatic experiencing, a type of therapy that uses the body to access healing (somatic refers to dealing with the body)
- EMDR (eye movement desensitization and reprocessing therapy), which doesn't require talking
- Sensorimotor therapy, which blends thought-based and body-based techniques
- Brainspotting, which accesses the deep parts of our brain using eye position
- Trauma-focused cognitive behavioral therapy (CBT), which uses CBT techniques in a trauma-informed way
- Ancestral and ancient healing practices facilitated by Black, indigenous, and people of color

Other somatic practices that can be supportive:
- Breathwork, a practice that uses the breath as a mode of processing and healing
- Yoga, including trauma-informed yoga where inner safety and choice is emphasized
- Intuitive movement, based on what feels natural and good to you
- Bodywork, such as massage or craniosacral therapy
- Dance, of all kinds
- Guided visualization and meditation

Willingness

In order to reckon with your story and really, truly reframe it, you must be willing: to let yourself shift, to not know, to do the work, to let it be easy when it's easy, to let it be hard when it's hard, and to try on new ways of being, seeing, and feeling in ourselves and in the world. Being willing encourages possibility. When we are willing, there is so much room to expand, grow, and shift—room to become more of who we truly are.

You might find yourself saying, "Of course I'm willing! Why wouldn't I be?" Willingness, however, requires us to go directly against the hard stories we've been carrying. To be willing, we must acknowledge all the ways we might be wrong.

To be willing is to be open, and to be open is to honor what is no longer working. To honor what is no longer working is to take a deep look at ourselves and our lives and, instead of leaning in to the defenses and excuses and reasons, simply acknowledge what needs to change. To change is to take the necessary steps. It's hard work, being willing.

Willingness is also brave work. Willingness involves courage. It means being willing to take action when inaction feels easier. It means being willing to make missteps along the way and sometimes even to fail. Willingness takes our continual attention, and intention, to allow new ways of being with ourselves to emerge.

Willingness can show up in small ways; your steps toward it don't need to be big in order to be meaningful. It can be as simple as choosing to make a therapy appointment or to read this book. It can show up in big ways, too—like being willing to leave a relationship that isn't supportive, being willing to be honest with yourself about your feelings, and being willing to take responsibility for your healing.

Safety: having a safe space, both within ourselves and with others, to explore, reframe, and integrate our story

Willingness: being willing to embrace a new, more supportive story

What might willingness look like in exploring your story?

- Being willing to face the potential pain that will arise in exploring your story
- Being willing to examine your story from different frameworks and lenses
- Being willing to shift the story you tell yourself through mindsets and practices
- Being willing to be with the challenges that arise while shifting your stories
- Being willing to let your stories go
- Being willing to release the grip on what you think you've known that might not be true
- Being willing to be honest about what arises with you as you explore your story
- Being willing to ask for help, support, and assistance when needed
- Being willing to experience the discomfort of change and growth

As you explore what willingness might look and feel like for you, it might be helpful to check in with what it will offer you. What is on the other side of doing this work? Why does it matter to you? How does this work impact you in positive and supportive ways? What inspires your willingness? Who models willingness who you can turn to when you need a reminder? How can you honor your willingness in small and big ways? How can you stay rooted to your willingness?

Four Supportive Mindsets

A gentle reminder: I hope you're feeling proud of yourself for seeking this understanding of how you can shift stories as they arise. It's such a gift to yourself, and even though we may not know each other off of these pages, I feel proud just thinking about you reading this.

Okay . . . onward.

Reframing our stories involves cultivating the mindsets necessary to show up in new ways. I hope this is a relief—to me it is—because it's a reminder that we don't need to reach a certain destination or get to a certain point. It is less of a singular process and more of an ongoing commitment to living into the truth that you are enough, as you are.

Mindfulness, curiosity, self-compassion, and aligned action are four mindsets that support us on this healing journey. They are mindsets that I center in my own life. At the beginning, embracing these mindsets takes time and intention—we must choose them over and over again. Over time, the mindsets become less of a choice than a habit. They become a way of being with ourselves and being in the world. (More on that in Part Three.)

The practices I share here have been deeply supportive and effective for me and my clients as we welcome these mindsets into our lives, but there are countless practices that people turn to for support. None of them are right or wrong—they're all valid, and what works for one person may not work for another. What's important is tuning in to recognize what feels supportive for your own unique context and needs. Notice how each of these mindsets might fit into your life. Notice the ways you've already practiced them without even knowing it. Notice where you might want to introduce these mindsets more intentionally, and imagine how they might support you in moving closer to who you actually are.

Mindfulness

You might have rolled your eyes when you saw the word "mindfulness." I get it—everyone is talking about it these days. The truth, though, is that it's widely talked about for a good reason: it has the power to transform so much of how we move through the world. Stick with me here.

A critical piece in reframing your story is being mindful—being aware of—what stories you are carrying, how they affect you, and when they show up. But when people think of those who practice mindfulness, they often picture a sage sitting atop a mountain, legs folded, arms crossed, eyes closed, in a moment of total Zen. The truth is that mindfulness is as simple (and complicated) as being present in the moment without judgment. We can all practice it, no mountain needed.

I first learned about mindfulness when I was in the hospital as a teenager, after I tried to end my life. Each day the other teens and I had to go to "class," where we would learn about topics related to mental health. One of the classes was on mindfulness. At first I shrugged at the idea of it—I didn't think it was for me. I thought of it as something reserved for more evolved humans (relatable?). As we talked about it in class, though, I learned that mindfulness wasn't so much about being in a Zenlike state; it was more about noticing what was happening for me in the moment. Paying attention. Witnessing. Observing. Recognizing the thoughts that were arising within me and, instead of obsessing over or criticizing them, allowing them to pass in natural time. Over and over.

From there, I read more and more about mindfulness from teachers like psychologists Tara Brach, Rick Hanson, and Shauna Shapiro, and Buddhist practitioners like Jack Kornfield, Sharon Salzberg, and Pema Chödrön. These teachers guided me in more fully understanding how mindfulness impacts our brain, how supportive it is for our well-being, and how helpful it is in being with the messy stuff *and* the beautiful stuff. I continue to learn so much from them.

I soon started practicing being mindful in other settings, in a variety of ways. I practiced witnessing my thoughts and naming them instead of immediately believing them. I practiced observing my thoughts as if they were a movie playing on a screen in front of me, slowly creating a little bit of distance between me and what was unfolding in my head. I practiced turning toward what was happening in my body. When going inward felt like too much, I'd practice tuning in outside of me: noticing my environment, scanning the room, using all my senses, picking colors to look for, paying attention to what I was hearing . . . Mindfulness outside our body can often feel safer when mindfulness within is overwhelming.

Practicing mindfulness in all of these ways supported me in creating a space between what happened and how I responded. Instead of responding from old stories automatically, I took a breath. Then I decided to respond from a new story. I remember once, early in my own healing journey, when a colleague disagreed with my opinion on something. The story that came up in that moment was from my belief of not being enough: "I won't be accepted if someone doesn't agree with me." Rather than responding from that story, I created a new one that honored myself: "I can be disagreed with and still accepted at the same time." By pausing before moving from my old story, I was able to engage in the conversation. Doing so led to a deeper connection in the midst of disagreement and created an opportunity to connect with my colleague that wouldn't have happened if I'd led from my old story. You can see how mindfulness allows us to engage with ourselves, others, and the world in ways that are generative instead of reactive.

The beauty of mindfulness practice is that it doesn't look one way. Every single human can implement mindfulness practice into their life in different ways (I've listed a few later). It can be used when we're feeling joy and when we're feeling deep pain. It can be practiced anywhere, at any time, for any reason (or no reason). It can be practiced with others or just within ourselves.

While mindfulness can be practiced in so many ways, its results are similar. It offers us a chance to pause before we react, to slow down before we jump to conclusions, to make space to notice what arises within us, and to have more say in the way we approach ourselves and those around us. And as we practice more and more, it becomes a way of moving through the world.

Mindfulness continues to be a way of moving through the world that I cultivate deeply in both periods of growth and periods of challenge. It's a way of moving through the world that I recommend to my clients, too. Inviting clients to tune in to what is happening in their body, to practice paying attention to their inner voice without judgment (often the hardest part), to slow down—these tools inform so much of how I teach clients to form a more intentional relationship with themselves—to listen to themselves—to start trusting themselves. When you've been moving through life for years without paying attention, mindfulness can feel challenging. It's important to normalize this—to know it's okay for mindfulness to be hard sometimes. I often think of things being hard as signs that we're doing important work, signs that we're embracing new patterns, new ways of thinking, and new ways of being.

What mindfulness might look like:

- Noticing when old stories resurface

- Paying attention to your reactions and responses

- Practicing awareness of your feelings and emotions

- Listening to bodily cues, needs, and desires

- Practicing nonjudgmental responding

- Pausing before reacting with automatic patterns

- Making conscious choices throughout your day

- Coming back to presence whenever possible

- Using your five senses to engage in life

Mindfulness can feel hard at first *because* it's difficult to try something new. Remember, our brain really likes when things stay the same. Mindfulness can also feel hard because when we finally start paying attention, we notice things we might have ignored, like discomfort or challenging feelings, sensations, or experiences. But with that comes the chance to show up for ourselves in new, more supportive ways.

You practiced mindfulness by choosing this book. Exploring your stories, deepening your understanding of how you've formed them, and gaining awareness of the ways you've been carrying them—this is mindfulness in action.

Ways to Implement Mindfulness

Slow Down

S l o w   d o w n. A short phrase that typically brings up a lot of anxiety. How do we slow down in such a fast-paced world?

Slowing down is an important way of implementing mindfulness because we can do so only by paying attention—by noticing our pace and recognizing when we're rushing, moving too quickly, or living from urgency. Our culture tends to reward rushing, quickness, and urgency; we are pressured to respond to emails immediately, get

---

A note about mindfulness related to trauma: if you have experienced trauma and find mindfulness or meditation particularly challenging, you are not alone. Paying attention to our pain can alert our nervous system, which often feels retraumatizing. If you've become accustomed to numbing or avoiding pain, focusing on your inner world can be overwhelming. Mindfulness slowly becomes more accessible, but doing so through a trauma-informed lens can be deeply supportive. David Treleaven, researcher and author of *Trauma-Sensitive Mindfulness,* is a wonderful guide to seek out if you need some gentler ways of paying attention.

back to people right away, and make decisions at the drop of a hat. Just because our world has become fast-paced doesn't mean *we* need to be rushed all the time, though.

One way I slow down is by being in nature often. When I go for walks or hikes or just put my feet on grass, I'm reminded of the natural rhythms that surround us. Nature doesn't rush, yet everything moves as it does. I'm reminded that I can create more natural rhythms within me. I can release that sense of urgency and embrace the idea that there is a time for the unfolding of what's meant to unfold. I've even noticed that if I go for a hike or just a short walk in the morning, the rest of the day feels more easeful for me. Something about witnessing nature leads me to slow down enough to witness myself—to remember my own nature.

When we slow down, we're less likely to rush our decision-making, responses, or actions, which makes it more likely that we will show up intentionally. This supports us as we reframe our stories, because when we slow down enough to recognize what's happening and what's arising in us, we get to choose how we want to respond. We can choose to live from a new story rather than an old one.

Slowing down can look simple—like taking a breath before answering a question or taking a break from social media. However you can implement it is wonderful and important. Where can you move a little more slowly? What tasks can you complete at a bit of a slower pace? What can you take off your to-do list? How can you find more slowness in your day-to-day life? In what ways might slowing down create opportunities to invite in new stories—new ways of being—new ways of living?

Another result of slowing down? Presence. The state of being completely and totally in the moment, without dwelling on the past or trying to predict the future.

Have you ever noticed that everything seems to become clearer when you are present? Like the clutter in your brain seems to more naturally organize itself when you are present instead of occupied by anything outside of the very moment you're in? The power of presence offers us beautiful opportunities to be with ourselves right here, right now.

Presence is challenging for many because being present means noticing everything that's happening, what's good and what's hard. It means being aware of how we are impacted by events and witnessing what's coming up within us. Sometimes that means noticing painful feelings. But with that, we have greater access to who we are *now*, not who we were. We can ask ourselves how we want to treat ourselves, how we want others to treat us, and respond from there. It is in the present that everything happens. It is in the present that we have room to decide how we want to respond next. The present holds power.

When you think about finding presence, I encourage you to explore what presence looks and feels like in your own life. How do you know you're fully present? What do you have access to when you are present? What gets in the way of finding presence? What makes it challenging, and what might make it easier? How do you think finding presence would support you in remembering the truth of who you are? In what ways might finding presence create opportunities to invite in new stories—new ways of being—new ways of living?

Encourage Gratitude

When we are present, we're more able to see clearly. We can find the sparks of joy, the moments of goodness, and the evidence that we are more than our hard stories. Cultivating gratitude helps us see these things even more readily.

Growing up, I was repeatedly told I should be grateful for being adopted. Sometimes I was grateful. Other times I wasn't. But it felt like I had to contort myself into a version of myself that was *always* grateful—even though I had been separated from the person who carried me and the lineage I came from. These experiences gave me a deep distaste for gratitude.

Gratitude is often talked about as a way to cover up what's hard—like when I felt hurt about losing my birth family. The phrase "Be grateful!" can be dismissive of our real lived experience and our actual feelings. I think of this kind of gratitude as forced gratitude, which is neither real nor sustainable. In fact, forcing gratitude can disconnect us from our truth even more, further enhancing the stories we're trying to release.

In graduate school, I started learning about the research around gratitude. I felt a harsh reaction to it at first because of my own experiences with forced gratitude. Slowly, though, I realized that gratitude isn't about being grateful for *everything* as much as it's about being grateful for *something*.

The powerful thing about authentic gratitude is that it isn't meant to cover up what's hard; it's meant to remind us of what is there *besides* what's hard. That's the *something*. It's meant to allow us to see what else is happening, what else is possible, and what else is true. It is mindfulness in action, really—being willing to pay attention to the good, the beauty, the joy that is already here when we slow down and are present enough to notice it.

Our brains are wired to see the negative—it helps us assess danger and survive. But life gets challenging when we're constantly noticing the negative. The practice of gratitude allows us to train our brain to move out of that bias and into noticing the good, too. This doesn't mean we have to force gratitude when it doesn't feel natural. What it does mean is that we have access to gratitude when we want or need it, and it is a resource and practice that can benefit our healing.

My relationship with gratitude has changed the way I approach myself and the world. It allows me to access awe and wonder—both of which are so important to me. It allows me to not get sucked into the narrative that everything is terrible when life feels hard. It allows me to remember the goodness that exists right alongside the pain. It keeps me grounded without denying the harder parts of being human.

What is your relationship with gratitude like? How have you practiced gratitude in the past? What perceptions or judgments come up when you think about gratitude? How might you introduce (or continue practicing) gratitude into your day-to-day life? In what ways might cultivating gratitude create opportunities to invite in new stories—new ways of being—new ways of living?

Curiosity

Curiosity is defined as a strong desire to know something. I see curiosity as a mindset that invites openness into our lives. Curiosity: an inner pathway to what's possible, and a pathway that I lead from in my life.

An alternative prompt if gratitude feels too difficult: "What is something I feel good about today?"

While mindfulness helps us pause to notice what stories we're telling about ourselves, curiosity helps us figure out *why* we're telling those stories. It helps us open up to possibility, to choice, to new perspectives, and to the magic and mystery of being human. Ask yourself questions that lead to personal inquiry. Explore different ways of viewing the stories you've created. Practice using a more expansive viewpoint as you look at yourself. That's how we can explore alternatives, new ideas, different ways of holding things, new lenses to view experiences through.

Curiosity helps us move out of our automatic patterns, which naturally invites different ways of showing up for ourselves. As someone who spent years of my life swimming in self-criticism, I found the phrase "get curious" transformative. When I think about embracing curiosity as a mindset, I ask myself questions. Here are some I think about and ask clients:

- How else can I interpret this?
- What else might be possible?
- What else could be going on here?
- What might I be missing?
- What might I have overlooked?
- How can I look deeper into what I'm experiencing?
- What would be a more easeful way of holding this story?
- I wonder what it would be like if _____ happened.
- How can I make space for something else to be true?
- Where might I be asserting fact when it could just be a story I'm telling myself?

Even asking these questions allows other ways of thinking and feeling to arise. Reading the questions creates the possibility for answers even if there are no answers yet.

Curiosity has allowed me to examine myself from different viewpoints, different perspectives, and different lenses, all of which teach me new ways of holding my experiences, beliefs, and stories. I think curiosity is a natural invitation to what else could be, which offers a glimpse of hope. It's a chance to see what living differently could be like—to live in a way that supports our wholeness and not just in a way that might be keeping us small, stuck, or stagnant.

Whenever (well, not whenever, but as often as I can, because hi, I'm only human!) I start telling myself an old story, I try to ask myself some of the questions I've listed on page 110. As I do, I start recognizing where I might actually be wrong. From here, I can show up for myself in a more supportive way, which totally transforms the moment.

Even recently. In my work, for example, I often share information in bits and pieces to help others further their own healing. For a long time, I was working on a course that would present this information in a different format. I hesitated to share it. I kept telling myself a story that it wasn't good enough—that I needed to make it better before sharing it (hello, perfectionism). Repeating this story kept me from sharing it for months and months. I noticed the story I was living from wasn't moving me forward, so I got curious. I finally allowed myself to ask some of those same questions. I asked: what *else* could happen if I shared the course? I thought it might help some people, even if it wasn't perfect. (And I'll say it again, nothing is perfect; no one is perfect.) I shared the course, and the experience is going way better than I anticipated. This is a very basic example, but it shows how curiosity can pave the way for a new story and a new way of living.

It sounds so simple, but infusing our lives with curiosity is a practice that doesn't always feel easy (because simple is rarely easy). When we practice it consistently, though, our minds start grasping

What curiosity might look like:

- Asking what *else* could be true

- Noticing what story you're telling yourself and asking why it might be there

- Utilizing different lenses to view situations

- Bringing in other points of view

- Exploring your sensations, emotions, and feelings

- Asking new questions and exploring alternatives

- Being willing to let things unfold differently

- Being open to something new unfolding

for new stories instead of clinging to old ones. We become more comfortable exploring instead of settling. Curiosity is the antithesis to stuckness and an invitation to possibility.

(By the way, you practiced curiosity by choosing to read this book. You followed an inkling, a wondering, a curiosity . . . nice work!)

Other Ways to Implement Curiosity

Embrace Wonder

When I think about the moments in which I experience wonder most often, I think of being in nature. When I'm in nature, I tend to observe everything around me slowly. I observe the way light reflects off of different surfaces. I observe trickling water and shimmering ferns. I observe how the wind sounds in different areas. I observe how different plants change each time I revisit the same spot. I wonder why. Later, I'll look it up online or ask a knowledgeable friend or read a book. I come to new insights through doing so. I see things in new ways. Wonder leads to new knowledge. It also allows you to practice not knowing—to accept that there may be things you'll never know—to stay curious about the unknown.

The same thing happens when we embrace wonder within ourselves. Wonder is about embracing the mystery, the unknown, the awe-filled, and the questions, and exploring with a curious heart. It's about nurturing what we might never fully understand. It's about witnessing the uncertainty with reverence. It's about honoring the depths within ourselves as magical and awe-filled. It's about seeing the miracle. When we embrace wonder, our old stories don't stand a chance. We create pathways that can lead us toward creating a new story and a new life. Wonder is a pathway to something better.

Exercise Choice

One of the most important parts of moving forward and showing up for ourselves in new ways is recognizing the choice we have in it all. Curiosity helps us remember the choices we have.

We can't automatically choose to feel a certain way. We can choose how we respond. We can choose what action we take. We can choose the story we tell about ourselves. You might feel like the way you respond to yourself is "just the way it is." The truth is that there are *so* many ways it could be. You can choose to say "It makes sense why this feels so hard" instead of "What's wrong with me? I shouldn't think this feels so hard!" You can choose to ask for help instead of trying to do everything on your own. You can choose to practice new habits instead of assuming you'll never change. You can choose to show up for yourself by setting boundaries instead of continually feeling resentful. We exercise choice in so many ways.

But this can be especially hard if you've had your ability to choose taken away in the past. It can be painful to give yourself permission to choose after feeling like you didn't have a choice for so long. If you had no choice but to stay small and quiet growing up, it might feel hard to remember you can choose differently now. If you had no choice but to keep your feelings to yourself, it might feel hard to realize you can share them now. If you had no choice but to be treated a certain way, it might feel hard to realize you can choose whether or not you allow it anymore. Lack of choice in the world around us can easily paralyze us into feeling like we have no choice at all.

Use curiosity to discover choices you might not have recognized before. For example, if you felt you had no choice but to stay small and quiet growing up, what else can you choose now? Are there ways you can choose to be seen and known? How could your choices support you in reframing your story? Get curious about the choices you want to make for yourself.

Practice Self-trust

Earlier, I mentioned being assigned a family tree in elementary school. I desperately wanted to include my birth mother on my tree, even without knowing her. She was a part of my tree, too. But when I told my teacher, she said, "You only need to include your real family! You only have one mom." I never told anyone about what happened.

That assignment left me feeling distrust for what I considered in my own tree. It went against my idea that I had a birth family out there and that they mattered to me. They did matter to me, even though I was told they shouldn't. I wanted to let them matter, even though I was told I shouldn't. I wondered what was wrong with me and began questioning my own beliefs, desires, and needs. Over time, I found it really difficult to trust myself at all. It's wild how a seemingly simple experience at such a young age could have deepened my lack of self-trust in such a potent way.

We all have moments like this. I imagine you can think of at least one example from your own life—a time when you were feeling something specific but were told that feeling was wrong, to push it away or to ignore it. These messages teach us to distrust our own intuition, wisdom, and knowing. Gaining awareness around why self-trust has been difficult for us makes it easier to begin developing it, even when it feels hard. When we remember that cultivating self-trust is a practice made up of moment-to-moment actions, we can start practicing it in ways that honor our own inner compass, needs, desires, and wisdom.

By validating my own inner experiences, as I shared in Part One,

I was able to honor my own truth instead of denying it—to accept my own feelings instead of hiding them—to trust my own responses instead of faulting them. Over time, and with ongoing practice, these small moments of self-honoring have led to a deeper self-trust. Curiosity requires that you ask questions about yourself, for yourself. Self-trust allows you to embrace where those questions lead you.

Like many of the other practices in this book, self-trust is a practice. It can be as simple as checking in with your needs and doing something to meet those needs. Pay attention to how you're feeling and validate it. Get clear on your beliefs and stick by them. Notice your inclinations, instincts, and intuition and choose to turn toward instead of away from them.

Self-compassion

Do you talk to yourself the way you'd talk to someone you love?

Many of us didn't learn to do this, growing up—we learned instead to criticize ourselves, internalizing the voices that might have shamed us.

Simply put, self-compassion is the act of showing ourselves compassion, even in the midst of challenge and failure. It's allowing ourselves the grace to be imperfect and not to let that mean we're bad. Dr. Kristin Neff has dedicated her research to this life-altering idea. She writes: "When we give ourselves compassion, the tight knot of negative self-judgment starts to dissolve, replaced by a feeling of peaceful, connected acceptance—a sparkling diamond that emerges from the coal." Alongside psychologist Chris Germer, Kristin has been a leading teacher in this work.

I didn't learn about self-compassion until I was in graduate school (that tells you how limited our access often is to this information). Then I studied all of its benefits: decreased anxiety and depression, increased motivation and ability to learn from mistakes, greater emotional resilience, and increased curiosity, to name a few. But I had an overbearing inner critic, so turning toward self-compassion felt challenging at first. You might find yourself questioning the compassionate response you offer yourself, too, if you're used to beating yourself up for every little thing. Since, again, we crave sameness and feel safer when things are comfortable (even if they're not necessarily good), continuing this practice takes consistency and dedication, even when it feels wrong.

At least that was how I felt. Slowly, I started noticing my inner critic with more intention. I began questioning whether or not I wanted to speak to myself that way anymore, and what purpose it was serving for me. I thought I'd get nothing done if I was always compassionate to myself—that I'd have no drive or willpower or ability to be productive. I thought my criticism was keeping me in line somehow. Like if I punished myself enough, I'd somehow do what I thought I should do. In grad school, this looked like telling myself my work was bad as a way of trying to improve. Or insisting I wasn't good enough as a way to try and get "better." The systems we live in replicate this "tough love" idea, too—we are taught to believe that being hard on ourselves and others leads to change.

Soon I realized we actually have *more* capacity for accountability and getting things done when we embrace self-compassion. When we create a sense of safety within ourselves, we're more likely to take risks; to do the things that matter to us; to try. Self-compassion supports us in creating that sense of safety: instead of knowing we'll get punished for being human, we begin with knowing we'll offer ourselves kindness and care, no matter what happens. You may be surprised at the results when you're not under pressure to perform.

One of the biggest, most transformational pieces of self-compassion is that it allows us to create a safe home within ourselves, which makes it safe to be wrong. To make mistakes. To mess up. To experience our flaws out loud. When we hold a well of punishment, criticism, self-judgment, or hatred within ourselves, we will do whatever it takes to avoid our own wrath. We'll do whatever we can to avoid the truth of being imperfect. We'll avoid conversations, hesitate to show up, turn the other way, and stay small. We'll hide from our own harm. But when we know we'll have our own back—when we know we won't punish ourselves—when we know we will remember our goodness even when we do something we wish we didn't do, or not know something, or lack awareness around something—it becomes so much safer to try. To learn. To take action steps. To show up. To do something. To engage. To keep going.

Self-compassion has become a cornerstone of my personal practice. It's one of the most important parts of my ongoing healing. I still have moments when I am self-critical (again, human here). However, self-compassion allows me to foster a relationship with myself that feels nourishing instead of punishing. It's particularly helpful as I reframe my stories. I might notice an old story arising, like "I'm not enough, so I need to stay small." Instead of getting mad at myself for momentarily giving in to my story of never-enoughness, I notice it (mindfulness) and ask myself what else might be true (curiosity). I then remind myself how hard it is when that story pops up. I remind myself I'm not the only one who sometimes forgets the truth of who I am. I tell myself I'm still good and enough, even when I forget. All of this is self-compassion. Offering myself compassion makes it easier to remember the story I want to live from—the story of being enough, always.

This practice has allowed me to separate from some of the messages I've received externally. It has reminded me that I don't have to stay stuck in old stories, that I can choose to talk to and treat myself in a compassionate way, which always feels better and more aligned with my values.

A beautiful side effect of practicing self-compassion is that it has also allowed me to practice a deeper compassion with other people. It's really hard to hold compassion for others when you're continually bashing yourself. It's hard to witness the humanity in other people when you refuse to see it in yourself. And it's hard to sit with other human beings and all of their stuff if you find it impossible to give yourself permission to sit with yours without letting it make you bad, wrong, or broken.

Starting out as a therapist, I had little compassion for myself. I made all of my sessions with clients another reason I wasn't enough. I criticized myself for messing up, hyper-scrutinized my "performance," and questioned every other word I said; all of this made it so difficult to be truly and fully present. This was unintentionally harmful to the therapy work I was doing—to put my own sense of self-assuredness in someone else's hands is a way of putting undue pressure on someone else to perform for me. How often do we use other people to measure our own worth? And how can we be present with other human beings when we're so focused on the ways we aren't measuring up?

Self-compassion transformed not only my personal life but also my work. I can honor my mistakes without calling myself one. And because I make room for my humanity to be acceptable, I'm now more able to fully experience the humanity of the person sitting across from me. I learned how to be with people without an underlying agenda and without unconsciously expecting my needs to get met from what occurred with them. A gift for me and for the people I work with.

Modeling self-compassion with clients is an important component of my work as a therapist. I respond to clients the way they deserve to be responded to in any and all of their experiences: with loving kindness, compassion, acceptance, empathy, and positive regard. So many of my clients didn't receive this kind of response growing up, and allowing it in the present can be somewhat uncomfortable. It seems so simple, yet allowing ourselves to receive compassionate attunement from another person is quite difficult when we haven't had it before. Normalizing this discomfort for clients and sharing about why it might feel challenging provides another layer of compassion—and as we engage from this place of kindness, there is an opening into possibility. A shift. A new story developing, a story of being enough, even when they mess up and sit in uncertainty and feel down—a new way of being.

Other Ways to Implement Self-compassion

Practice Radical Acceptance

Pain + resistance = suffering: a Buddhist saying I first heard from Tara Brach.

For most of my early life, I resisted the pain that came with being adopted. I shoved it down deeply, as if that would make it go away. Although I didn't know it at the time, resisting my pain was actually making it worse. Resisting my pain made me feel wrong for feeling it in the first place, which led to shame, which led to feeling even worse about my pain. Can you see how quickly the cycle of pain and resistance stops us from accepting our humanity? We cannot have compassion for things we do not accept.

I remember sitting with a therapist in a residential treatment center I stayed at for a few weeks when I was fifteen, after being hospitalized a second time. The therapist was talking about

What self-compassion might look like:

- Talking to yourself the same way you would talk to someone you love

- Acknowledging when things feel hard for you

- Validating your feelings and emotions

- Offering yourself support and reminders

- Giving yourself permission to make mistakes

- Letting there be room for learning and unlearning

- Having your own back

- Offering yourself gentle touch

- Recognizing that you aren't the only one and other people experience what you do

allowing—allowing my pain, allowing my feelings, allowing my story. One of our practices for that week was to notice and allow, notice and allow, notice and allow . . . repeat. It felt strange to me. Wrong, even. Why would I allow sadness and disappointment and grief and shame? Why would I be okay with them? I wanted to do the opposite. I wanted it all just to go away. *I* wanted to go away.

My therapist began sharing about how when we resist our pain, it gets swept under the rug. But what's under the rug often grows and worsens until it's out of control. Instead, he suggested that nothing—not pain, not any feeling—should be swept under the rug.

That therapist was the first person to teach me about what I now know is radical acceptance. As we explored the idea, I thought of how so many people around me did the same thing I did—trying to fix or minimize what I was feeling, emphasizing that I should "just be grateful," putting positive spins on pain, not asking how it was affecting me. I wasn't the only one pushing away what hurt; so many others were pushing away my hurt and their hurt, too. So few of us know how to be with what hurts.

The practice of radical acceptance is the practice of allowing all parts of us to be okay, even when they don't necessarily feel okay. It's the practice of honoring both the light and the dark, both the pain and the joy, both the ease and the challenge. Tara Brach, who wrote a whole book about it, calls radical acceptance "the willingness to experience ourselves and our lives as it is." What a shift from pushing it all away, running from it, or denying it. What a way of being with ourselves.

Let's say, for example, you are going through a breakup. You might be feeling pain, grief, and self-doubt. You might be wondering what's wrong with you or why it didn't work out or how you could have fixed it. You might find yourself resisting the feelings that arise within you by talking shit about your ex, or going out for drinks more often than you might normally, or feeling an increase of self-criticism that seems unrelenting.

What would it be like to notice and allow what you were feeling? To witness your feelings with compassion instead of criticizing their presence? To honor your feelings without pushing away? To trust that you can manage your feelings from a place of compassion—that you can sit with them for longer than you may know? To accept what is?

Doing so is exactly what radical acceptance is about.

Radical acceptance might look like saying:

- "This is what I am experiencing right now, and perhaps this experience is okay."
- "I'm feeling a deep sense of grief, and maybe it makes sense. Maybe I can be with this feeling just a little bit longer."
- "I fully accept what is happening, and I don't need to resist it to feel differently."
- "I will not resist this feeling. I'll let it be here, too."
- "I'm aware of the emotions arising in response to this experience, and I own them fully."

Radical acceptance allows us to *be with* what we experience. When we practice acceptance of what has happened, who we've been, what we've done, and what we've experienced, we aren't saying it's all okay, but we *are* saying we'll no longer fight, resist, or deny it. Nothing goes under the rug. Acceptance of what *is* usually allows us to see we *can* change. Carl Rogers, a humanistic psychologist, said, "The curious paradox is that when I accept myself just as I am, then I can change." I believe the same can be said for our hard stories: when we accept our hard stories, we can start changing them.

Jen, my client who struggled with perfectionism, did just that.

She started implementing radical acceptance by shifting the way she saw herself through moments of imperfection. Her practice was to notice when her inner critic appeared. That inner critic got louder when she wasn't doing something up to her standards of perfection—like when she got a B on a test instead of an A. Instead of immediately believing her inner critic, Jen practiced accepting her mistakes. She practiced naming her experiences for what they were instead of cataloging them as evidence that she was not enough as she was. She didn't like her missteps; that's not what radical acceptance is about. But she allowed her missteps to be a part of who she was, and she learned to view them without so much judgment. Radical acceptance helped Jen live with her missteps and her successes. It helped Jen live into her wholeness instead of continuing to strive for impossible perfection.

Engage in Forgiveness (of Yourself and Others)

What is your relationship with forgiveness like? Who and what have you forgiven, and what did that look and feel like for you? Who or what are you still unable to forgive, and what does that look and feel like for you? Are there places in your life where forgiveness might create some freedom? Are there places that you aren't able to forgive right now (or ever) but might want to foster some acceptance instead? What might support you in doing so?

I held on to anger, confusion, and contempt for so long in many ways: toward my birth mother who abandoned me, toward those who didn't understand how to help me work through my adoption, toward circumstances that I didn't choose, toward myself . . . toward life. The act of forgiveness toward each of these took support, patience, and time, but forgiveness (over and over and over again) is what allows me to move forward.

Forgiveness can be tricky, though, because the urge around for-giveness tends to be "forgive everyone" and easily gets confused with "have no boundaries and allow everyone a seat at your table." I don't believe we have to say "I forgive you" out loud. I don't believe we even have to offer forgiveness to those who have deeply hurt us. I don't think it's a requirement for healing. What I do believe is that practicing forgiveness is less about being okay with everything and more about accepting everything. You can't change what happened, but you can decide some of what happens next. That's how forgive-ness can help you show up from a new story. It has reminded me that *here* is where I want to be, and that putting my attention and care on cultivating the life I want is more supportive than always replaying the things I wish didn't happen.

What forgiveness might look like in your life:
- Leaning on empathy and compassion for yourself and others
- Setting boundaries for yourself about what's forgivable and what's acceptable
- Exploring the choices you have in the present
- Finding meaning in what has happened
- Accepting the past while consciously creating the future
- Leaving behind what no longer serves you, even when it's hard
- Making room for grief and honoring all your feelings
- Cultivating a forgiving mind, over and over

Practice Surrender

No longer forcing. No longer trying to control. Releasing your grip. Embracing what is. Trusting in what hasn't become yet. Surrender is a deep way of practicing self-compassion, because it requires us to accept what we are instead of trying to berate ourselves into being different. And here is where I find practicing surrender most helpful as I reframe my story of never-enoughness: it reminds me that I am enough, as I am. It allows me to soften into my humanity. In Buddhism, nonattachment is a core part of easing suffering, which is deeply related to surrender.

Surrender reminds us that there is only so much we can do; there's only so much we have a say in; there's only so much we can determine. It supports us in creating spaciousness around our experiences instead of gripping tighter to what we can't control. It gives us the opportunity to breathe—to honor what is—to find ways to stay with ourselves through whatever we may be experiencing. Sometimes we need to let go of trying to make everything go a certain way and make room for things to unfold as they do. We are only human, after all.

Surrender doesn't mean we stop trying. It means we honor what we do have a say in while letting it be okay not to know, not to control, and not to force. Letting go sometimes breeds forgiveness; it often breeds acceptance, and acceptance breeds surrender, all of which fuel and are fueled by self-compassion.

What surrender might look like in your life:
- Not trying to control all the outcomes
- Letting go of old stories and the belief that they must be true
- Making room for the unknown to unfold
- No longer forcing, gripping, or trying to determine everything
- Balancing your power with your sense of trust
- Releasing the need for certainty
- Embracing the unknown

Aligned Action

Mindfulness, curiosity, and self-compassion allow us to understand the stories we've been carrying and explore the stories we'd like to carry. Aligned action allows us to live into new stories.

Something I hear so often as a therapist is "What should I do with all this information?" When you're ready to take action, it usually means you've done some processing first. In the case of reframing your story, processing means you have understanding and awareness of how your story came to be, you've explored ways to find compassion and acceptance for that part of yourself, and you're ready to practice new ways of being with yourself, with your *full* self.

With my story of not being enough, I first needed to understand where it came from. I then needed to cultivate mindfulness to notice when that story popped up and how it affected me. I needed curiosity to explore what else could be true, and I needed compassion to remind myself how challenging it is to move through these stories. With that information, I needed to start choosing something different—choosing a story of being enough, just as I am.

This looked (and continues to look) like reminding myself that my old stories aren't true— they're just stories, and I can choose to tell myself more supportive ones. It looks like doing the thing I want to do instead of listening to the story that I'm not worthy of it. It means allowing myself to receive support instead of listening to the story that my needs are too great. It means getting up and getting a glass of water when I'm thirsty. It means going for a walk when I need a reset. It means doing the things that are good for me even when I don't want to. It means regularly practicing all the mindsets

I've shared about in a way that supports the truth of my enoughness. Aligned action is about recognizing who we really are, what we really need, and what we really desire, then taking the actions necessary to support those things.

What aligned action might look like in your life:
- Going to sleep when you're tired
- Showing up and being seen, even when part of you doesn't want to
- Spending time with people who value your full self
- Repeatedly telling yourself new, more nourishing stories about yourself
- Making choices that support your well-being instead of falling into old habits
- Putting your phone away instead of doom-scrolling (spending endless time scrolling on Instagram or Twitter, even when it isn't making you feel good)
- Asking yourself what you need and then doing that thing
- Exploring your values and then taking action based on those values
- Practicing all the things that support you in coming home to yourself

Aligned action is challenging because no one can tell us exactly what it will look like in our lives. I'm just as often asked, as a follow-up: "What *exactly* should I do with all this information?" The fixation on finding that answer often stops us from understanding all the small incremental actions that lead to new ways of being. There isn't one answer. We want one fell swoop when what leads to change are the moment-to-moment actions we choose to take. We're programmed in our culture to look for the big change, the quick fix, the end goal, and the monumental shifts. The normalization of this way of viewing change makes it difficult to trust that change actually happens in tiny, incremental, momentary choices—one after the other, over and over, for the rest of time. This doesn't sound nearly as alluring as being able to share a "before and after" photo does.

What's more, these actions often require us to do things we don't necessarily want to do and push through discomfort. They require us to care for ourselves in ways we might not be used to—to show up for ourselves in ways we might not always trust we deserve—to center what we need over what we want at times—to truly listen to ourselves—to be in an ongoing relationship with who we actually are and to act from that place. The discomfort that comes from showing up for ourselves is worth it, though. The beauty of aligned action is that it leads to honoring your inherent worthiness, goodness, and enoughness. When we continuously engage in aligned action, we start to bring new stories to life—we act from stories of being enough, of being worthy, of being lovable, of being whole.

Other Ways to Implement Aligned Action

Engage in Gentle Discipline

At the residential treatment center I was in at age fifteen, where I first learned about mindfulness, one of our daily assignments was to complete a journaling exercise. I hated it at first. I hated writing when I didn't feel like it, I hated the idea of feeling obligated to do something and to do it over and over. I wanted a quick fix. All I wanted was for what I was experiencing to just go away, fast.

Through journaling every day, I slowly noticed changes. I noticed myself thinking more openly about my feelings. I noticed myself pausing to explore what was coming up for me more frequently.

I noticed myself having a better grasp over what was underneath my external behaviors or thoughts. The practice of journaling gave me an opportunity to regularly and consistently come back to myself, as challenging as it was at times. After a while, I even started looking forward to the daily practice, not because it felt great but because keeping the commitment to myself was healing.

Discipline is a core component of healing. James Clear, author of *Atomic Habits*, shares widely about the importance of habit formation and the powerful impact building habits has on our overall life. Habits don't just form. New routines don't just create themselves. New ways of thinking don't come naturally. We have to work at them, put in the time, and commit ourselves to do so over and over again. For those of you who grew up with inconsistency, lack of structure, and uncertainty, discipline might feel even harder because it wasn't modeled for you. If you didn't have a bedtime, you might have the story that discipline doesn't matter. If you were allowed to do whatever you wanted, you might have the story that you can't be disciplined. Because, as I shared earlier, we internalize messages we grow up with, these stories can affect the way we care for ourselves as adults, whether or not we realize it.

Cultivating discipline is a way of reparenting ourselves. When we do for ourselves what wasn't done for us or what we've always wanted to do but couldn't, we remind ourselves that we are worthy of care.

Note that discipline can become unhealthy when it falls out of alignment with what we actually need (for example, not leaving room for flexibility, leaning in to perfectionism, not honoring our own cues, bypassing our needs for the sake of discipline, et cetera). It isn't about being harsh on ourselves, pushing ourselves when we actually need rest, trying to dominate how we're feeling, or punishing ourselves when we fall off track. Real, gentle discipline is a gift. It's a way of holding ourselves accountable as an act of self-love. Mindfulness helps us discern the difference.

What discipline might look like:

- Choosing to follow through on your commitments to yourself
- Staying engaged in practices that are supportive
- Implementing and practicing nourishing habits
- Caring for yourself even when you don't want to
- Making choices that align with your needs even when they don't feel good
- Actively staying connected to your own healing
- Practicing consistency, over and over

Take Radical Self-responsibility

The hard part (well, one of the hard parts) about growing up is that we become our own responsibility. We can understand why we're hurting . . . we can rationalize why we feel the way we do and why we behave the way we do . . . we can hold our experiences within us . . . but if we want to heal, we can no longer continue blaming, projecting, or displacing our own responsibility for our lives. I say this with as much gentleness as possible (it's a struggle for me, too).

When we no longer hold anyone else accountable for how we show up for ourselves and how we show up in the world, we can ask:

- How am I contributing to the continuation of stories that no longer serve me?
- In what ways am I afraid to take responsibility over my life?
- What would it feel like to claim responsibility over my choices, feelings, and beliefs?
- How was self-responsibility modeled (or not) for me growing up?
- What feelings arise within me when I think about taking responsibility for my life?

- Where might my own responsibility be lacking, and where does it feel strong?

These questions are no easy exploration. I avoided them for a very long time. I fully understand why so many of us still struggle with taking full responsibility for ourselves as adults—especially if we didn't get what we needed as children. It can be painful to recognize the fact that it's our job now.

Radical responsibility means choosing to have a say in our life no matter what. We will never be able to fully control what anyone else does, what happens in the world, or what the future holds. What we can control is how we respond to what happens within and around us.

That idea resonated with my client Jasmine as we dove deeper into her story. Jasmine was used to catering to other people's wants and needs, but she slowly began to identify what she wanted and what she needed: more space to offer herself the same care she offered everyone around her. She wanted to change her story from needing to be helpful to proving her worth, to knowing she's enough without being helpful. Her wants and needs mattered, even if she wasn't being "good."

This took a while. Reframing our stories is often a lengthy process because our brain has become comfortable with familiar ways of thinking, feeling, and being. And new doesn't feel natural. With time and practice, though, it got easier. Jasmine investigated where her beliefs came from. This alone was transformative. Whenever her old story came up, she practiced saying to herself, "Oh, here's this story again." This created some distance between her and the story . . . which allowed her to slowly recognize that she wasn't her story. We dissected her story until it was just that—a story. Jasmine was eventually able to see that her story of being worthy only when she was helping wasn't true. It was just what she once believed, and for good reason.

From there, Jasmine and I collaborated on new ways she could show up in relationships. We got curious. We explored how to understand what her needs were and how to name them with others. Jasmine practiced radical responsibility by reminding herself that only she could make the necessary changes to honor her needs. No one else was going to do it for her. Once she did, she found opportunities for small shifts. She started and ended her days with self-reflection, which eased her anxiety. When a friend called or a coworker asked for help, she paused to consider if she had the time and energy to offer help in that moment. She said yes or no depending on her own assessment. Taking radical responsibility supported Jasmine in claiming her rightful space in her life. This changed how Jasmine showed up in her relationships. This was radical responsibility in action. When we no longer attach our well-being to anyone outside of ourselves, we have more capacity to heal. We no longer give in to old patterns. We remind ourselves that we are in charge of our choices. We honor ourselves.

What radical self-responsibility might look like:
- Choosing to do the hard thing that's good for you instead of the easy thing that isn't
- Taking responsibility for how you respond to the world around you
- Showing up for yourself when you commit to showing up for yourself
- Honoring what's happened and choosing what's next
- Taking full responsibility for your healing (this doesn't mean you have to heal alone)

- Being honest with yourself, even when it's difficult
- Owning your choices, actions, and emotions

I want to clarify that practicing self-responsibility doesn't mean we don't get to ask for help or support from others. And it doesn't mean we aren't allowed to be frustrated and upset when others let us down. It also doesn't mean that we shouldn't be impacted by the systems we live in. Instead, it means we can recognize the ways we are impacted by other people and by external systems while *also* choosing the way we want to respond to those experiences. It's a both/and situation: we can both be impacted by things that are not our responsibility *and* take responsibility for how we show up for ourselves.

Make the Next Best Move

I've found that many people hold off on taking aligned action because they feel they can't see the big picture yet. They don't know where things will lead, or what the outcome will be, or how their lives will change. There is fear involved in taking action, which can easily cause us to retreat into old patterns, habits, and stories. The thing is, we don't need to know everything that's ahead. We just need to focus on the Next Best Move.

The Next Best Move is about taking things one step at a time. In exploring change, it usually feels much less overwhelming to ask, "What's the next best move?" than it does to ask, "What do I have to do over the next two years in order to get to where I want to go?" One keeps us present and engaged; the other keeps us overwhelmed.

It isn't usually the big changes that lead to new ways of being . . . it's the little moves we make day to day. These moments, combined, create our life. Our culture highlights instant gratification as the norm and makes it easy to want quick fixes, so it makes sense why it might be challenging to trust the bigness of small, tiny choices . . . but discounting the next right move as too small to be significant ignores how impactful our everyday actions are.

What the Next Best Move might look like in your life:
- Trying one new thing instead of ten new things
- Paying attention to and meeting your daily needs
- Focusing on the here and now instead of the long term
- Noticing the things you're already doing
- Recognizing the small actions as mighty and important
- Finding meaning in moment-to-moment shifts
- Reminding yourself you don't need to have it all figured out

Exploring the Next Best Move gives us only one thing to do at a time, which is way more doable than changing everything all at once. When I was writing this book, it looked like asking, "What's the next paragraph going to look like?" instead of asking, "How am I going to write an entire book?" With living into new stories, it might look like asking, "What's one action I can take today in support of honoring my worth?" instead of "How can I feel worthy all the time?" Instead of asking, "How do I live into a new story?" it might look like asking, "What's one way I can honor this new story I'm cultivating today?" It's really about taking what we want and distilling it down to actionable steps, which, over time, leads to big, beautiful change.

A gentle reminder: Okay, that was a lot.

Here's a great place to take a breath, roll your shoulders, stretch your arms up to the sky, and check in with yourself. How are you feeling? What is arising within you? How is it feeling to take in this information and explore how it relates to your own unique context and life? Checking in with yourself as you move through this book is a way of not just consuming it but really thinking about how you might want to apply it to your life. Thank yourself for doing this work. It matters.

Ways Discomfort Might Arise

As you consider the stories you are shifting and rewriting, I invite you to ask yourself what might change with the mindsets of mindfulness, curiosity, self-compassion, and aligned action. How might these support you in remembering what stories you want to carry and what anchors you while you do so? Returning to these mindsets is transformative, powerful, and healing in itself.

This can feel hard—it can bring up feelings of frustration (*Why do I have to do something with it?*), sadness (*I wish I didn't have to do this hard work*), guilt (*If I'd just figured this out a long time ago, I wouldn't be in this position*), grief (*I've wasted so much time, and I'll never get back what I've lost*) . . . it brings up a lot, so please know it's absolutely normal and even okay to feel whatever you may be feeling.

I repeat: **your feelings are valid.** I can't tell you how many times—often a day—I repeat this to myself as a reminder that it's okay to be human.

Because here's the thing: it *is* hard. Anything new is hard—even if it's good for us. New means uncomfortable, and uncomfortable means not what our body or brain is used to. Remind yourself that you will, and should, feel discomfort at times. Especially when it comes to reframing our stories. It means something is moving—shifting—changing.

Next, I've listed some ways in which you might encounter this discomfort. I think of these as road signs on our healing journey—they may slow us down, but they shouldn't stop us. Being aware of signs along the way helps us recalibrate when they come up instead of veering off course. These experiences aren't "bad"; they offer information for us to explore. Instead of asking, "How do I get rid of this?" you can ask, "How do I want to relate to this?" See what it feels like to welcome these signs—what it feels like to embrace the discomfort before pushing it away.

Resistance

Have you ever avoided or resisted change? If so, you are not alone, and there is nothing wrong with you—change can be so scary when we're used to the way we've been carrying on for so long.

When resistance comes up in my own life, I remind myself of past times when the very same feelings arose and I kept moving through them anyway. I recall saying to myself, "I can't do this at all" when I started graduate school, but I kept going anyway. I remember telling myself, "I'm not going to find out anything, so what's the point?" when I took my Ancestry.com test, but I took it anyway. In my practice, I see resistance when clients describe their stuckness, their difficulty implementing new patterns or behaviors, or even when they disregard their deservedness of joy. We resist when we aren't sure how to live into new ways of being in the world. It doesn't mean we don't want to—it just means we aren't always sure how and even if we can.

Normalizing, even validating, this reaction can be an integral piece of healing because our tendency is to push resistance away

Resistance may sound like:

"I don't want to do this."

"I can't do this—it's too hard!"

"I'm going to try this another time."

"I'm going to do the easy thing
instead of the right thing."

"I know what I need but I'm going
to do something else."

"I'm going to skip my walk today."

"This is all pointless and stupid."

or question it or deny it . . . all of which are, ironically, forms of resistance. Instead, we can honor the part of us that doesn't want to change, even as we seek change.

Another way to think about it: In *The War of Art,* Steven Pressfield says, "Remember our rule of thumb: The more scared we are of a work or calling, the more sure we can be that we have to do it. Resistance is experienced as fear; the degree of fear equates to the strength of Resistance. Therefore the more fear we feel about a specific enterprise, the more certain we can be that that enterprise is important to us and to the growth of our soul. That's why we feel so much Resistance. If it meant nothing to us, there'd be no Resistance." This quote has been a meaningful anchor to me in exploring resistance because it points to what's underneath it—and beyond it. When we recognize that we're resisting change, we can practice getting curious about why, instead of berating ourselves for what we're experiencing. Why might we feel afraid? What might be on the other side of that resistance? How might resistance be a part of this journey rather than something to try and bypass?

As you reframe some of the stories you carry, I invite you to notice any kind of resistance that arises within you. Is there a part of you that doesn't want to let go? Is there a part of you that feels attached to your stories? Is there a part of you that wants to keep the stories you've held for so long because of how familiar they are, how comfortable they are, or how connected you are to them, even as they limit you? If so, you are not alone. Those parts of you get to be there, but they don't have to decide what happens next.

Questions to explore resistance:
- When does resistance come up the most for me?
- What does resistance feel like in my body?
- What thoughts usually accompany resistance?

- How does resistance impact my ability to take action?
- What information might resistance have for me?
- What supports me in moving through resistance?

Fear

As Steven Pressfield indicates, along with resistance typically comes fear. Fear often signals that we're doing something out of our comfort zone, something new, or something different. Along this path lies risk but also opportunity—as Pressfield reminds us, fear is also an indicator that what's at stake really matters to us.

Remember, like all forms of discomfort, fear is a sign. Fear is not always a red flag; it can be a guidepost that marks what we are called to do, change, or be. Fear is something to pay attention to, because here's the thing about it: We can't get rid of it. We can't avoid it. We can't live a life without it, because it helps us survive! It has allowed us to look both ways when we cross the street, to not text while driving, to lock our doors, and to make sure we don't get into other potentially harmful situations. Fear is necessary and good. The tricky thing is when we allow fear—without asking questions of it—to dictate what we do or don't do. If we allowed fear to stop us from doing things, we'd probably get very little done. We'd never pursue relationships. We wouldn't go after jobs we want. We wouldn't share our art. We wouldn't hike or perform or travel or do anything new. When we understand fear as a natural part of being human, we get to feel it and do things anyway.

Explore your resistance and fear from a place of friendliness. Resisting resistance amplifies resistance (say that three times fast). Fearing fear amplifies fear. However, seeking to understand, even

Fear may sound like:

"What if something goes wrong?"

"I hate not knowing what's going to happen!"

"If someone doesn't like this, everything will be bad."

"I don't know if I can handle this."

"How will I survive if things don't change?"

"It's too scary to do this new thing."

"I'm not capable."

"I'm just going to mess up."

welcome, these aspects of change allows them to exist without over-powering us. When resistance or fear pops up, say hello to it. Ask it what it might be wanting to tell you. Notice what sitting with that answer feels like. And, as you allow it to be there, see what it's like to continue anyway. To keep showing up for yourself regardless of whether resistance or fear shows up (because you can guarantee they both will, ongoing, forever).

When resistance or fear decides to visit, remind yourself that it's normal, it's okay, and ask yourself what you need to keep moving. You can let resistance and fear know that while they might be present in your choices, they don't get to lead the way. They don't get to choose for you.

From that place, we can make changes that might feel scary, but only at first.

Questions to explore fear:
- What fear is arising right now, and why might it be here?
- What does fear feel like in my body—when do I know it's here?
- How can I pay attention to my fear without getting persuaded by it?
- What supports me in discerning between fear and danger?
- How might fear be pointing me toward what matters to me?
- What supports me in moving through fear?

Loneliness

Choosing to untangle the stories we've been carrying often means we will show up differently in the world . . . and that shift will be experienced by the people around us as well. Not everyone in your life may want you to change. Some people might even be threatened by it, especially if your old stories benefited them in some way. If you are letting go of a story of needing to be small and you start taking up more space in your own life, then people who got more of their needs met by your smallness might feel uncomfortable. Say, for example, a friend used to spend most of their time with you talking about their own life and their ups and downs. When you show up from your new story, prepared to take up more space, you may want to talk about your own life and experiences, too. That friend might not like getting a little less space in the relationship because they're used to having more. When your stories change, your relationships might change. Changing relationships isn't a sign you're doing something wrong—it's a sign that you are listening to what you need and honoring it, even if it means your relationship won't look the same. Remembering that this isn't always a bad thing makes it feel less challenging.

When we're used to relating with others from our old stories, it makes sense why we may not be able to do so in the same way as we change, grow, transform, and return to who we truly are. You might find yourself distancing from people and places and spaces that don't support your growth, and spending more time alone. You might feel lonely. I want to normalize the feelings of loneliness that might arise as you reframe your stories and care for yourself in a new way.

Ask yourself if the loneliness you are feeling is because you are actually alone, or if it's because you are allowing yourself to take the time and space needed to look deeply at what is working and no longer working for you in your stories, your relationships, your life. If it's the latter, this kind of loneliness can be a sign that you are allowing yourself to decide whether the company you keep is honoring your full self and, if not, that you get to choose whether or not you

Loneliness may sound like:

"It's like no one knows the real me anymore."

"It's hard to let go of relationships that
only had room for my old stories."

"It's lonely to feel like no one understands
what I'm moving through or how hard I'm
working to become more of myself."

"I wonder if I'll ever connect with anyone
from this new place I'm in."

"I want to feel truly seen as my full self."

want to continue keeping that company. In turn, you get to decide what kinds of company you want to keep moving forward and what kinds of relationships you want to have. And, if you are indeed really alone, what lessons are held even in that loneliness? What can be gleaned from being alone? What might it point you to, make more clear, or move you toward?

Questions to explore loneliness:
- When does loneliness tend to arise most commonly?
- What feelings come up when loneliness is present?
- How can I discern between loneliness and being alone?
- Who can I connect with when I'm in need of connection?
- What meaning can I make of loneliness when it arises?
- What supports me in moving through loneliness?

Confusion

Showing up for ourselves and others in new ways can be deeply confusing.

Confusion is a sign that we are entering into unknown territory—whether that's a new relationship, a new job, a new habit, a new story, whatever. How we relate to our confusion is more important than attempts to conquer it. When growing, stretching, and trying something for the first time, you won't have all the answers. Instead, I encourage you to ask questions. When confusion arises, how do you want to greet it? ("I'm not sure what to think here, but I'm going to welcome this sense of confusion and see what it has to say.") What might it be needing from you? ("Knowing confusion is here, what do I need to remind myself of? What might I need

Confusion may sound like:

"I feel like I don't know who I am anymore."

"I don't recognize myself."

"I'm not even sure what I want."

"I have no idea where this is heading."

"This is all so unfamiliar."

"Am I doing this right?!"

"I feel so lost."

to hear in order to be okay with the confusion? How can I support myself through the confusion?") What might you be needing from it? ("What don't I know yet, and is that actually okay? What might bring me more clarity? How can I be with this confusion instead of trying to get rid of it immediately? What do I need to do for myself while confusion is here?")

When we view confusion as a part of change, and a hallmark of growth, it becomes less scary. It becomes part of our process. It becomes an invitation to deeper understanding.

Questions to explore confusion:
- What does confusion usually need from me?
- When does confusion come up for me most?
- What can I remind myself when confusion arises?
- What information does confusion have to offer?
- What supports me in moving through confusion?
- How might confusion help me gain clarity?

Discomfort may come in other forms for you. What's important is that you can welcome these big feelings. They can be signs instead of roadblocks. They have something to teach us, too. They contain lessons and value also. In a society that prioritizes positivity over just about anything, it's important to remember that discomfort is also part of being human—that it's not always something to fix. There's no need to get rid of it, only to shift how you relate to it when it comes to greet you.

As you explore moving through discomfort, I encourage you to lean back into the mindsets I mentioned earlier in this section. How would mindfulness support you in noticing when discomfort arises? How might curiosity encourage you to explore discomfort instead of being cowed by it? How might self-compassion allow you to be gentle with yourself in moments of discomfort? How might aligned action allow you to choose what route you want to take when discomfort comes up? This is a place to implement these mindsets. It's a place to remember that you have a say now.

Exploring how various practices might support you in moving through discomfort can be nourishing, too: What would it look like to practice radical responsibility in managing discomfort? What would it feel like to engage in radical acceptance when discomfort comes to visit? How would it help if you brought in surrender during moments of discomfort? Navigating discomfort by using some of what you've discovered (or rediscovered) in this book is such a beautiful way of remembering your power and putting it into practice.

Other Ideas, Mindsets, and Practices That Support the Reframing Process

Inner Wisdom

A natural result of all this inner work is a deeper belief in what we know . . . a deeper knowledge of what we need . . . a deeper sense of what we want. It slowly becomes easier to trust ourselves. Something that is really powerful to witness with clients is the transition from asking *me* for answers to listening to *their own* answers. Slowly, clients begin realizing they can trust themselves—that they know just as much as I do. Their inner wisdom is worth paying attention to.

Writing new stories invites us to rely on that inner wisdom instead of what we've been taught, what's been expected of us, and what others have wanted from us. It's how we remember ourselves.

It's how we return to ourselves. You are not only your hard story. You are so much more.

Reconnection to the wholeness of who we are doesn't mean we become perfect or even good. It doesn't mean forgetting about what has happened, ignoring our pain, or denying what hurts. It does mean recognizing we deserve joy, connection, and self-acceptance, too. As long as we're alive, each day brings another chance at telling ourselves a more nourishing and supportive story, one that allows us to show up in our lives, messy and whole at the same time.

Knowing what you know now about the stories you've carried, what do you want for yourself? What do you need? What stories would you want to fill yourself with?

Answering these questions helps cultivate a relationship with our own wisdom. It's a way of recognizing the knowledge we've always held within us but didn't always have access to. By remembering all we already know within us, we get to be the expert of our own lives.

Practices:
- Before asking for someone else's opinion, advice, or validation, see if you can get still and connect with yourself. What is your opinion? What advice do you want to receive? What validation do you need, and can you give it to yourself?
- How do you feel when you know something? What signals does your body give you? What senses ignite? What supports you in tapping into your own knowing?
- What foundational beliefs do you carry? How do you let them inform your choices, connections, work, values, actions, and ways of being?

Inner Child

With mindsets, practices, and a deeper sense of inner wisdom, we create a greater capacity to tend to our inner selves in small and big ways. Some of the most profound inner work I've done both personally and professionally is inner-child work. "Inner child" sounds like an out-there term for many, but getting familiar with our inner child is a major part of moving through our hard stories and embracing our wholeness. In psychology, the inner child is defined as the parts of us that represent our younger self, which often had needs that went unmet or unseen, that we still carry within us. Dr. Dick Schwartz, the founder of internal family systems therapy, an evidence-based modality of psychotherapy, teaches that our selves contain various parts, of which the inner child is one. Every single one of us has an inner child. And our inner child can lead us to where we need healing.

I often think back to my eight-year-old self. I was eight when I found out I had been abandoned. I never talked about it until I went to my first therapist. I held the pain, confusion, and grief of abandonment all on my own for so long, desperately wishing someone else would see it and understand. The version of myself who needed to be told that it was okay, who needed to be validated and heard and seen, has been within me all along.

I tell my inner child now what she needed to hear then: that it makes sense why she felt alone, that she didn't need to be fixed. I remind her that she isn't alone and she's still good. I let her know she was meant to be here—that she isn't a mistake. I connect with that younger part of myself often, and every single time, it heals. Given that many of our hard stories form in childhood, this kind of work can be so helpful as you uproot, unravel, and rewrite what no longer serves you. When we connect to our inner child from a place of feeling grounded in the present, it can transform our relationship with ourselves and other people.

Prompts to connect with your inner child:
- What did you need to hear growing up that you didn't hear?
- What did your younger self love doing, and what did you feel when doing it?
- When did you have to abandon your needs in order to maintain connection?
- What ages did you experience the most challenge in? What did you need then?
- What was it like for your younger self to experience what they did?
- How might you connect with your younger self now, and how do you notice when younger parts of you are present?

Inner Parent

Tending to the needs of our inner child requires that we access our inner parent. I (and many others) think of showing up for ourselves in this way as reparenting—caring for ourselves the way we wanted or needed to be cared for growing up, and recognizing our ability to choose to do that now. I have my own back. When you have yours, you are parenting yourself, in a way.

Our inner parent is the part of us that is responsible for our well-being, entirely. Our inner parent is the part of us that knows how to care for our needs in a compassionate and loving way, even when we don't necessarily want to. Treating ourselves the way we need to be treated instead of the way we have been treated in the past, and responding to our experiences, feelings, and emotions the way we wish others did, allows us to practice calling on our inner parent. Reparenting doesn't always mean doing what feels good; it's also very much about doing what feels necessary, which sometimes means going to bed early even though part of us would rather stay up late and watch another YouTube video.

Connecting with your inner child and inner parent creates an opportunity to do things differently—and that's what I mean by living from a new story.

What might this look like? you ask.

Let's say it's the first day of a new job, and you're experiencing a big emotion, like fear. Your old story of not being enough might arise and sound like: "You shouldn't even bother trying. No one is going to like you. Stay small. You're afraid you aren't good enough, and you're right." Maybe, as a kid, you heard similar things. Perhaps you were often told to suck it up and get over it instead of sharing this kind of big emotion. So today, years later, your inner child is activated. This is where reparenting is so supportive—you get to show up for yourself in a different way now. You get to remind yourself it's okay to feel that big emotion. You get to tell yourself you deserve to be where you are. You get to offer yourself the support you needed then, now.

You can access your inner parent by giving yourself what you actually need. You know that you're enough, as you are. You might say: "It's okay to feel afraid. It makes sense why you might feel scared right now. What do you think you need to move through this fear? What can I remind you of right now? How can I support you in this moment?"

Having this inner dialogue with yourself might feel weird, I know. But acting from this place, rather than from your old story, creates an entirely different response to fear, or to any big emotion, obstacle, or challenge. It allows you to do the thing you want and need, even when it feels hard.

My inner parent is so supportive when I feel indifferent or hesitant toward doing the things I need to do to take care of myself. That looks like drinking enough water, choosing to go to bed when I'm tired, scheduling a doctor's appointment if something feels off, taking personal responsibility for my life, and reminding myself of my values in order to stay connected to them. It looks like doing my laundry even when I don't want to, knowing it will make my life easier. It looks like eating a full meal when I'd rather not eat. These are just a few examples of what leaning on an inner parent can look like. You might not use this phrase, but the meaning of caring for ourselves in the ways we needed, and continue to need, remains.

Can you think of examples when your inner child shows up? What about your inner parent? How might you tap into these parts of you more intentionally? What would change through creating a relationship with these parts of you?

Exploring Values

"I used to value making sure everyone else was okay—how I looked—how successful I was—how I appeared to others—whether or not I did things right. I'm not even sure what my values are now, because I've been living by what I thought they *should* be for so long." This isn't a real quote, but I know so many of us have experienced something along these lines.

As you grow and change, and rid yourself of old stories, you may not be sure what's left when you do—what's left of you. Something I've found to be so insightful, helpful, and supportive is to reconnect to your values.

When I ask people about their values, they often can't name them. What frequently comes up first are the values they've been conditioned to have or the values they've witnessed around them,

Examples of values:

Creativity, acceptance, ambition,

dependability, giving, honesty, playfulness,

commitment, skill, responsibility, trust,

uniqueness, fairness, justice, kindness,

mastery, respect, power, openness, passion,

spirituality, hope, integrity, transparency,

connection, solitude . . . to name a few

which aren't always aligned with who they were or who they are now. I imagine this is true for many of us.

Acceptance and commitment therapy (ACT) is a type of therapy that explores values, or the qualities we choose to honor and pursue, and helps people live in accordance with these values. This process is empowering because we often inherit the values of those we were raised by, of the cultures we were raised in, and of the society we've grown up in, all of which may or may not be the values we would choose for ourselves. Similarly, your values may have been different when you were living from old stories, which is why returning to this exploration now is so important.

When you're thinking about values, it can be helpful to explore what's important to you and what brings you meaning:
- What values do you hold sacred?
- What values guide what you do and how you show up in the world?
- What values feel resonant with who you are right now?
- What values do you find important but aren't yet living by, and how might you introduce those values into the way you live?
- What values resonated with you in the past but no longer feel aligned?

Explore your values. Write them down. This can be a clarifying, even eye-opening practice. Some of my values are integrity, creativity, connection, presence, freedom. When I explore these values and check in on how I'm living or not living from them, I get more insight into what I might need to shift. When an old story of wanting to stay small arises, I can ask myself, "Will this cause me to disconnect and live outside of my value of connection?" It can be a pragmatic way of reminding ourselves what's important to us. Values can be thought of as guideposts—when I lose my way, I look to my values to guide my actions. I revisit my values a few times a year to see if they're still resonating with me and if I want to identify new ones. Integrating values work into your life is such a wonderful practice—I hope you find it to be so, too.

What Is and Isn't Ours to Carry

Reframing the stories we no longer want to carry often leads us to recognizing what was never ours to carry in the first place. This is even truer, in a number of ways, for folks who are marginalized, folks who don't fit into the status quo, folks who don't have as much privilege, and folks who aren't seen in their full humanity.

We live in systems that program us to think a certain way and believe certain things. Systems like patriarchy, white supremacy, and capitalism influence the way we're raised, the way our parents were raised, the way our grandparents were raised. Systems dictate who gets what and who doesn't—who gets access and who doesn't—who gets support and who doesn't—who gets accepted and who doesn't—who gets believed and who doesn't—who gets admired and who doesn't—who gets their basic needs met and who doesn't—who gets safety and who doesn't. These systems also affect how we feel about ourselves and our bodies, and other people and their bodies. It affects how we feel about what we "should" be doing, how we "should" be acting, what's deemed right and wrong, what's deemed normal and not normal. These beliefs can grow into stories. Stories about who you should be, what you should do, what your identity means about who you are as a person, what your skin color means about your worth, what your sexuality means about your goodness, what your faith means about your belonging, what your size means about your importance, what your location means about your intelligence . . . I could go on. We have inherited these stories from the systems we live in, and recognizing where these stories came from creates an opportunity to look at what's *actually* ours to carry and what we want to choose to put down. People like Sonya Renee Taylor, Audre Lorde, Angela Davis, Desiree Adaway, Rachel Cargle, Rachel Ricketts, and so many others have and are doing incredible work in teaching about these systems and the ways they impact how we live, both internally and externally. Talking about how we've all been programmed while living within these systems is deeply painful and disturbing but eye-opening. Recognizing and then understanding what isn't ours to carry is a process many of us become more aware of as we talk about these systems. Movements, activists, and groups all over are doing the brave work of speaking out, standing up, saying "no more," and putting themselves out there in order to change these systems. Many have been doing this work for decades. It's awe-inspiring and rage-inducing and a reminder of how much work exists outside of us in order to change the systems that have caused so much pain within us.

As you move into reframing the stories you no longer want to carry, it's important to identify the ones that were never yours to begin with. Externalizing the expectations, pressures, norms, rules, standards, judgments, projections, ideas, beliefs, ideologies, structures, labels, and boxes so many of us have been put in without our consent makes it easier to see what doesn't belong to us. The world may not always like it, but we were never meant to abandon ourselves in order to meet the standards that weren't created with our wellness, and wholeness, in mind.

For your exploration:
- What stories have I attributed to me that aren't actually mine?
- Whose expectations and labels have I internalized?

- How am I still carrying the programming I've internalized elsewhere?
- What am I making a me problem that is actually a systemic problem?
- What am I taking responsibility for that isn't mine?

Moving into Possibility

Reframing your story takes work, but with it comes an abundance of opportunity. If we're creative and capable enough to create and believe the hard stories we've carried about ourselves for so long, we are also creative and capable enough to conjure up and believe something else might be possible. Muse on this for a moment before you continue.

Let it be possible.

I wrote this in my early twenties while I was grappling with who I was and who I wanted to become. I was right in between an old story and a new one, trying to balance on wobbly ground. The old story had me pulling back and questioning if showing up for myself in a new way was possible, if I even deserved it, or if it was going to happen. The new story was trying to quiet the old story and pull me back into the truth of myself. In that moment, I remember having a conversation with myself. It went something like this.

"I don't think I can do it. I don't think I can become the person I'm wanting to become."

"Let it be possible."

"But what if it doesn't happen?"

"Let it be possible."

"What if I don't deserve it?"

"Let it be possible."

"I'm always going to be this way."

"Let it be possible."

"I don't know how to let it be possible!"

"Let it be possible."

"What if I stay stuck and depressed and alone?"

"Let it be possible."

"Fine. Maybe it's possible."

Several years ago, I took a solo trip to Joshua Tree and spent six days alone in the desert, trying to remember what was possible. To many, this sounds terrible—and to be honest, part of it was. Being forced to confront yourself isn't always the most pleasant or comfortable experience—it isn't what most people picture when they imagine a solo vacation. But I was at a point in my healing journey where I needed to find space for myself to just be myself.

I drove the eight hours from the Bay Area to Joshua Tree. "Strangest Thing" by the War on Drugs (an epic song) started playing right when I passed over a hill and entered into the desert. *Perfect timing,* I thought. As I listened to the music, I was awed by the sandy desert rose hues, Joshua trees lining Twentynine Palms Highway, dirt roads rumbling under the tires of my car. When the song ended, I noticed a piercing quiet I had never experienced before. Windows down, I felt the sticky heat on my skin. I knew this place was holding something important for me to discover. Majestic and quiet places always do.

What happened next wasn't what I expected. I got settled into my Airbnb, taking in the unfamiliar surroundings. I put down my bag, sat on the bed, and immediately started to cry. It wasn't a sad cry or a happy cry; it was a tired cry. I knew this cry. It was informing me that I needed to let go—of old stories, of ways of being with myself that didn't align with what I believed, of versions of myself I thought I needed to be—I was ready to release all of it.

During the next six days, something clicked. I finally felt parts of the new stories I was working so hard to integrate being rooted a little bit deeper within me. I felt myself more fully forgive my birth mother. I forgave myself for experiencing depression. I felt an ease enter my heart and suddenly trusted my goodness a little bit more. I experienced a deeper sense of trust in all I didn't yet know instead of the fear I had felt for so long when I was desperate for answers.

What felt most important, though, was the sense of possibility. I understood how possible it was for me to remember who I was underneath the stories of never-enoughness. I understood how possible it was for me to cultivate aliveness, even with my history and experience of depression. I understood how possible it was to change, over and over, even when I felt fear or hesitancy.

This trip helped me imagine my true self in a way I never had before. It solidified my desire to continue living into new stories— into stories of worthiness, of being enough, of embracing my full humanity, of letting my true self be seen, and of no longer wishing I was someone or somewhere different. By carving out space to really be with myself after doing so much healing work, I was finally able to see how all that work had helped bring me back to my own truth. I was finally able to trust how possible it was to keep going—to keep unlearning—to keep cultivating stories that honored who I was.

When we go through the journey of understanding and reframing our stories, we gift ourselves the possibility of remembering who we truly are. We create the opportunity to live from *that* place—to realize we have the power to shift out of old stories and choose how we want to live, be, and show up. The work of reframing our stories is difficult. It takes grit and commitment, patience and humility. It takes constant reminders, continual remembering, and repeated

Possibility might look like:

- Recognizing the variety of choices you have

- Holding space for what could be

- Looking beyond limitations

- Honoring your capacity to grow, shift, move, and change

- Exploring what you want and going after it

- Remembering that more is always possible

practice, over and over. But when we make the choice to take the journey of coming back home to ourselves and taking off the stories that no longer fit, everything becomes possible.

And when everything is possible, the ebbs and flows of doing this inner work are more than worth it.

Questions I might explore with clients around possibility (you can explore them in your journal, with your therapist, or in a casual conversation, if you're into that kind of conversation, like I am):

- What have I felt was impossible that is now a reality in my life?
- How does impossibility protect me or keep me feeling safe in some way?
- What do I wish were possible that I 100 percent know is not, and how can I find acceptance in that?
- What am I not sure is actually impossible that I am claiming is?
- What would it be like to make more room for possibility?

Carrying It Forward

As you arrive here, I invite you to recall what you've learned (or remembered) so far.

You've learned about how our stories come to be. You've explored how they show up in your life, and why they make sense in your own unique context. You've examined which stories are no longer serving you and which stories you might be ready to slowly release from your grip. You've been introduced to various mindsets, practices, and ways of being with yourself. You've learned about why reframing our stories can be so powerful. Now you get to explore what stories you want to carry forward. Now you get to explore what's possible. I hope you're proud of yourself for doing this work and diving in—I am proud of you.

We are the creators of our lives. It's really hard to believe that before gaining the perspective I hope you found in Part Two. The truth is that we get to choose who we are. We get to choose how we care for ourselves and how we show up in the world. We get to say, "I understand where those stories came from and how they showed up. It makes sense that they came to be. I have more knowledge of how I can cultivate new ways of being with myself and make room for who I truly am—and I'm willing to do what's needed to make it so."

When we go through the journey of understanding and reframing our stories, we gift ourselves the chance to rediscover our own enoughness. Moving from "I am not enough, I am unworthy, and I am a mistake" to "I am always enough, I am always worthy, and I am meant to be here" has allowed me to live into my truth. So . . . who are you truly, underneath the old stories you've been carrying and sifting through? Who are you before others told you who you are? Before you got assigned an identity by someone or something else? Before the labels, roles, rigidity, masks, facades, pretending, covering up, hiding, shoving down, shrinking, denying, shaming, conforming, contorting, fitting in? Before you began obeying the rules of who you were "supposed" to be? Who are you at your core?

You might not have an answer, and that is totally okay. These are questions we're not often asked. Your you-ness is waiting for you to claim it, though. Through the honest work of reckoning with your own stories and the brave work of beginning to reframe and release them, we give ourselves the opportunity to finally come face-to-face with our truth—often for the very first time.

- What stories do you want to carry within you from here on out?
- What stories do you want to continue rewriting and living into?

- What stories feel aligned with your wholeness and goodness?
- What stories feel empowering, supportive, and nourishing?
- What stories allow you to be exactly who you are?
- What stories give you the biggest opportunity for acceptance and compassion?
- What stories feel right? True? Real? Genuine?
- What stories describe the person you want to continue being—the person you already are?

Before we move into Part Three, I invite you to pause once again. Notice any sensations in your body, any thoughts forming, any stories emerging . . . and wrap your arms around yourself. Give yourself a hug. A squeeze. An offering of acceptance and a reminder of your own presence. I am honoring you from afar. Let's continue.

GETTING FREE

INTEGRATING OUR STORIES

For a long time, I couldn't imagine myself being anything other than hurt. I was so used to feeling that way, part of me didn't want to consider that I could be any different. Being hurt became my identity. To heal would be to undo so much of who I believed myself to be. Undoing, unlearning, and unraveling felt almost as terrifying as staying stuck in that identity. I see this mirrored in so many of my clients. I see it in so many of us—this hesitancy to allow ourselves to heal, to know we're deeply worthy of it, to know we deserve it.

I chose to heal, even though it's scary at times. I named my stories. I tried to understand them, and then I set about rewriting them. "I am not worthy" became "I am worthy just as I am." "Something is wrong with me" became "I'm just hurting." "I don't belong" became "I always belong." "I'm not lovable" became "I am inherently lovable." Slowly, I was able to live into the truth of who I am. "I'm not enough" became "I've always been enough."

I continue practicing everything I've shared with you in the book to this day. I will practice for the rest of my life. This is what it means to integrate our stories—we incorporate all we've learned into our lived reality. In neuroscience, they often say, "What fires together wires together," meaning what we repeatedly do creates new pathways in the brain. Living into new stories isn't as simple as saying them out loud—we must adjust our reactions, choices, relationships, beliefs, mindsets, practices, habits, and patterns, over and over.

Integration moves us from practicing new ways of being with ourselves to embodying new ways of being. According to *The*

Merriam-Webster Dictionary, to be embodied is "to give a body to." In this sense, we are giving our body to new stories. When we show up in a way that honors our worthiness, we slowly embody that worthiness. When we show up from a place of being good enough, we start to embody feeling good enough. When we engage in practices that reflect caring for ourselves, we begin embodying the belief that we deserve to be cared for. Embodiment means that although we might occasionally question or forget (because we're only human), we really believe in our worthiness and enoughness. That's how new stories extend their roots deep within us.

The rest of this section will explore what's possible when we lead integrated lives, what we're capable of when we live from our truth, what can support us as we do, and how doing so changes not only our own life but the communities we're part of and the world we live in. When I imagine every human living from their enoughness, I imagine a better, more connected, more beautiful world for all of us. I imagine this often.

There are so many things that can be supportive in this process. I will be sharing a few of them, but I invite you to also go within and explore what might not be covered here. You know you best, after all. What helps you stay aligned to your truth? What supports you in remembering what matters to you? What keeps you anchored in yourself? Honor what you know about yourself. Give yourself permission to name it as such and thus to live from it.

A few questions to consider about healing and integration:
- What hesitancies, fears, or doubts arise when you think about growing and healing?
- What are your thoughts about your own deservedness to heal?

- What does it look like to live into your worthiness?
- What does healing mean to you personally? What does it look like?
- How would you know you were healing? What would feel different?
- What have you discounted that might actually be healing for you?
- What stories are supporting where you are in healing at this moment?
- What stories are you choosing to live into, starting now?

Ways to Integrate Your Story

Choosing Rituals

A ritual is anything done meaningfully and with intention repeatedly, whether it's lighting a candle at night or pulling a tarot card in the morning. Rituals invite moments of pause and contemplation—all of which are opportunities to connect our intentions to our actions and integrate our stories of worthiness, goodness, and enoughness. Ritual has been an important part of healing in so many cultures for centuries, and it is something that has been somewhat lost in Western culture. Ritual has also been pushed aside as we move further and further away from connecting with the seasons and cycles of nature, which are inherently a part of us. Learning about what ritual looks like in other cultures, as well as what staying connected to seasonal living looks like, is a beautiful way of remembering the roots of humanity—the old ways that have nurtured and supported people since the beginning of time. Reconnecting to ritual in a way that feels nurturing and meaningful for us is a gift to ourselves.

What rituals might look like:

- Stretching each morning
- Lighting a candle or incense when you wake up or before you fall asleep
- Making a cup of tea and practicing presence throughout the whole process
- Pulling a tarot or affirmation card or intention each day
- Engaging in moon circles or ceremonies
- Making space to practice breathing exercises in the middle of the day
- Having a regular writing practice in order to engage in ongoing reflection
- Repeating a mantra to yourself once a day
- Following the pulse of seasons
- Pausing before eating your meals to notice how you're feeling

One of my favorite rituals is pulling a tarot card each morning. And it's not about predicting the future. Each card represents an idea—the Ace of Swords represents new beginnings, for instance—and as I look at the card, I just notice what comes up for me; how it connects to what I'm feeling; how it might inform the way I show up that day. It's so simple, but those few minutes of being with the card provide me space to pause and contemplate. The cards really just point us back to ourselves.

Rituals can change with the seasons, with different phases of our lives, when different needs arise, and when our schedules shift. What's most important is using these rituals as a way to check in with yourself.

A ritual doesn't have to be complicated to be meaningful and nourishing. What's one small ritual you might want to implement into your life during this season? What rituals feel supportive for you? What are you already doing that you might want to create a ritual of?

My client Jen asked herself these questions, too. She discovered one of the rituals that supported her in moving out of perfectionism was extending gratitude to herself each day. It didn't matter when or how, but every day she committed to listing three things she appreciated about her messy, fully human self. Building in this ritual allowed her to practice self-acceptance, which is an antidote to perfectionism. What started as a ritual quickly became a way of showing up for herself differently.

Jen allowed herself to show up imperfectly and in her full humanity outside of our sessions. She went to school without curling her hair every day. She stopped sharing only the highlight reel on social media. She finished projects without needing to fix one. more. thing. She enrolled in a dance class and allowed herself to be a beginner. She connected more genuinely with friends, which deepened her relationships. Through practicing all these things, she was able to see that she didn't need to strive for perfection to feel worthy and good enough—she just needed to trust that she already was those things.

Jen's story gently moved from "I'm worthy only when I'm perfect" to "I'm worthy always—even when I mess up." Releasing herself from the grip of perfection gave her permission to try new things, share how she was actually feeling, and have compassion for herself when she made mistakes; it gave her room to fail without being a failure. It set Jen free.

Jen is a perfect example of what liberation from our stories can create for us: freedom, yes, but space, room, and a lightness that causes us to live, connect, and love more fully. It wasn't that she never felt tendencies to be perfect, but understanding her old story, reframing it, and integrating a new one helped—a lot. In other words, healing didn't need to be another thing Jen did perfectly. We don't need to be perfect at living into our new stories; we just need to allow ourselves to be fully human, show up anyway, and try again. Jen stopped giving up when it wasn't perfect, and she kept trying, over and over. Doing so gifted her the wholeness that perfection kept her from feeling—the wholeness that she was looking for all along.

Setting Routines

While rituals create moments of pause and contemplation, I think of routines as commitments to actions that allow us to be well and whole. They're about doing what needs to get done. Tapping into our inner parent is supportive when engaging in routines—the part of us that knows what we need and takes responsibility for meeting the need in ways that support us. Routines can be as simple as eating breakfast at the same time each day, or planning a weekly menu to avoid stress. While we need room for flexibility around our time, introducing routine to our days/weeks/life can be incredibly supportive. Some folks need more routine than others, and depending on your schedule, routines will look different. The important thing is to turn inward to explore what a healthy and sustainable routine might look like for you in this season. Our routines can ebb and flow, but committing to a routine is a beautiful way of honoring your time and your needs.

What routines might look like:
- Going on a daily walk before looking at your phone
- Doing a meditation when you wake up
- Meal-prepping on Sunday evenings to create ease in your week

- Answering emails at certain times of the day
- Making a quick daily to-do list before you eat breakfast
- Carving out time in your schedule for daily tasks/chores
- Having a date with a friend once a month

When I was deep in depression, I didn't get out of bed until at least 10:00 a.m. This meant I didn't eat breakfast until I was starving, which meant I felt overwhelmed while trying to figure out what to eat, which made it harder to feed myself. Which made everything harder, in fact. You can see how being out of certain routines can throw us off and, on the flip side, how routines can deeply support us in living in alignment with our worthiness, goodness, and enoughness.

Rituals and routines can be both simple and impactful. The most important aspect of each is considering your needs and finding sustainable ways to meet those needs throughout your week. Rituals and routines offer us ways to practice consistency, which is a key part of any process of healing—continuing to show up, even when it's uncomfortable and even when it doesn't necessarily feel good. When we engage in rituals that nourish us, we remind ourselves we're worthy of that, which reinforces our story of worthiness. When we engage in routines that support our well-being, we remind ourselves we're deserving of the things that make us feel good. When we implement rituals and routines into our daily lives, we take action that aligns with how we are wanting to show up for ourselves. Going for daily walks gives me a place to reflect. Putting nourishing oil on my face in the evenings signals to me that I am worth taking care of. All the rituals and routines I engage in support me in integrating stories of worthiness, goodness, and enoughness. They signal that I am worthy of being intentionally and regularly cared for. I've found these practices to be a nurturing and intuitive

Instead of this:	Try this:
Checking your phone first thing in the morning	Journal or stretch before reaching for your phone
Mindlessly checking your emails throughout the day	Set certain times to mindfully check when you're able to
Having no plan for dinner and getting too hungry to think	Plan a few meals to ease stress and nurture yourself
Waiting until you're exhausted to slow down and rest	Schedule in time for rest throughout the week
Staying seated in the same spot throughout the day	Make it a point to get up and move your body regularly

way to continue living into stories that align with my truth. Finding what this might look like for you could illuminate new ways of being with yourself and new ways of honoring the stories you're currently living into.

Making Room for Joy, Play, and Ease

When old, painful stories weigh us down, we can find it challenging to access our joy, sense of play, and air of ease. Leading with our hurt becomes normal, and it's what we often see around us. As we reframe and integrate new stories, one of the most potent results is greater access to our natural birthrights: joy, play, and ease. We can forget we even have these parts of us.

If you lived in a story of feeling like you needed to earn rest, play, or ease, it might have been hard for you to intentionally make room for these things on a regular basis. If you spent most of your energy contorting yourself in order to belong, you might not have felt much lightness. If you were disciplined and play was taken away as a punishment, you might have felt like it was a luxury instead of a necessity. But when we slowly understand our worthiness, goodness, and enoughness, we more naturally realize how deserving we are of cultivating the things that bring us joy—the spaces we can experience play—the ways we can bring more ease to our lives. Unlearning hard stories can allow you to more deeply know this. You start recognizing that these things don't need to be earned, even when old stories told you otherwise.

Imagine your child self—the self who existed before you inherited and created beliefs about who you were or who you thought you needed to be. Think of your inner child—the younger parts of you that perhaps didn't get to express themselves through joy, play, or ease.

- What was younger you like?
- What did they enjoy?
- What mattered to them?
- What made them laugh hysterically?
- What excited and delighted them?
- What was their energy like?
- What would they have loved to do?
- What did their expression look like?

Those parts of us still exist within us. As we live into new stories that make room for all of our humanity, we naturally make more room for these parts of us that we've lost touch with. Connecting to and cultivating joy, play, and ease has been one of the most meaningful aspects of my healing: remembering my love of nature, my wild bouts of laughter, my endless curiosity about the world and others. Living into a story of worthiness, goodness, and enoughness has allowed me to bring these aspects of myself back to life. I squeal when my husband brings home ice cream. I color with colored pencils just for the sake of putting pencil to paper. I go on walks and notice all the little details around me. For so long, these things seemed like they were for everyone else but not me. Not anymore. Creating stories that center on joy, play, and ease supports me in staying connected to all parts of myself, even when old parts of me hesitate or question whether or not it's okay.

Someone who inspires me deeply when it comes to making room for play, joy, and ease is author Elizabeth Gilbert. She regularly shares the art she makes just for fun; the small things she notices in everyday life; the wonders that exist in the world; the delight that envelops us when we let go a little bit. Identifying expanders— people like Elizabeth Gilbert, who model what it could look like to live into these parts of you—is a powerful way of reminding yourself it's possible to do so.

Joy might look like:

Laughing a little longer than usual, dancing to your favorite song, savoring a good meal, wearing your favorite outfit just because, being totally present to goodnesses in your life . . . what would you add?

Play might look like:

Rolling down a grassy hill, coloring, creating, doing things just for fun, trying new things, engaging in activities that make you feel alive, practicing presence, losing track of time, laughing, lightheartedness . . . what would you add?

Ease might look like:

Letting it be easy, receiving support, doing what you're good at, accepting when things go well, slowing down, allowing life to flow, honoring what is, planning . . . what would you add?

I invite you to take inventory of what joy, play, and ease feel and look like for you:

- What brings you the most joy?
- How do you make room for play?
- What does ease look like for you?
- Who are you at your core—underneath all your roles?
- What brings you the wildest experience of wonder?
- What awes you?
- Where do you feel a hint of magic?
- What activities cause you to lose sense of time?
- What spaces invite a lens of newness and exploration?

Committing ourselves to prioritizing joy, play, and ease is a radical act in a world that so easily disregards it. The mere idea might feel really challenging right now, but I hope that through exploring these questions, and tuning in to see what comes up for you, you'll get a clearer picture of how you might be able to let these parts of you take up more space in your life.

Prioritizing Pleasure

Deeply feeling into positive experiences.

Allowing yourself to receive pleasure in all forms.

Making ordinary moments special in some way.

Engaging in activities for the sake of enjoying them.

Listening to music that evokes good feelings.

Finding luxury in small ways.

Pleasure comes in so many forms. When we prioritize it, we prioritize our own enjoyment. The more we do this, the deeper our stories of deserving pleasure become.

For many years, I wouldn't do anything special for myself. I'd do

Prioritizing pleasure is a way of honoring your capacity to feel good.

the bare minimum and nothing more. It was as if feeling pleasure seemed out of reach or only for the select few. The truth, though, is that I just didn't feel deserving of it.

As I live into my goodness, worth, and enoughness, pleasure has become an important part of caring for and honoring myself. I notice that when I take a few extra minutes to make my meal look beautiful on the plate, the experience of eating dinner becomes special. When I stop and smell a flower on a walk, it becomes sacred. When I hug my husband a few seconds longer than normal, it feels nourishing. When I use a special face mask on a Tuesday night just because, it feels luxurious. These little ways of infusing pleasure into day-to-day life continue to affirm that I am worth the regular experience of pleasure, without earning it, period. We all are.

What is your relationship with pleasure like? What comes up for you when you read the word? How have you been conditioned to view pleasure? How was prioritizing pleasure modeled (or not modeled) for you? What kind of person do you think deserves a life of pleasure? What do you imagine pleasure could look like in your life?

In *Pleasure Activism,* the author adrienne maree brown explores how pleasure is a personal revolution in itself—especially in a world that doesn't encourage it or make it easy to access. Her book has taught me so much about the radical nature, and power, of pleasure. Exploring how you might bring more pleasure into your life, whether physically, emotionally, sexually, spiritually, or in any form, is such a solid way of shaking up any old stories that said you weren't worthy of it. When we make pleasure a regular part of our life, we're also integrating the stories that allow us to know we are so deeply worthy of it.

Embracing the Mess

The process of understanding and reframing our stories is what allows us to recognize, shift, and live into our wholeness. It provides us with opportunities to choose what we can and embrace what we have no control over. It offers us a framework with which to live moment to moment, day to day, with more intention and care. What it doesn't do is erase the messiness of being human.

At no point will our lives be seamless, predictable, perfect, complete, flawless, or free of challenge. Sometimes old stories will pop up.

Something I talk about a lot (and give myself pep talks on) is embracing the mess instead of constantly trying to get rid of it.

What do I mean by this?
- I mean not letting the messiness of being human make us bad.
- I mean letting ourselves not get it right every time.
- I mean remembering who we are when we forget our truth.
- I mean knowing perfection or completion was never the point.
- I mean understanding our goodness amid the messy bits.
- I mean seeing our full humanity instead of zeroing in on harder moments.
- I mean letting ourselves laugh when shit hits the fan in totally unexpected ways.
- I mean honoring the fact that we are forever learning and unlearning.
- I mean recognizing when we're living from old stories and getting curious instead of critical.
- I mean forgiving ourselves when we find ourselves being critical instead of curious.
- I mean letting the process of creating new stories not follow a clear, outlined path.

- I mean knowing there will be seasons of ease and seasons of challenge.
- I mean allowing messiness to be a part of our humanity instead of something to shame ourselves for.

Embracing the messiness of life requires that we stop using our missteps or mistakes as proof that we're a failure. It means being willing to move through the uncertainty and the unknown without judgment. It means knowing life is never meant to be or look one way but is instead ever changing and often unpredictable. It means letting it be okay that our old stories pop up sometimes instead of assuming that's a step backward. It means letting go of our constantly expanding expectations in order to fully be with what is. It means knowing we are enough, just as we are. I remind my clients of this often, particularly Jen.

"Wow. I didn't think I would ever let myself be seen like this," Jen said in a session one day. She had explained that, at the beginning of our time together, she had lied—she'd said she was happy even when she wasn't. Now she was crying. "It's so hard for me to let you see me like this." Jen found sharing the truth of who she was incredibly difficult. I praised her for her courage. I let her know how common it is to want to hide the parts of us that we've deemed wrong or bad or broken. I reminded Jen that it's usually the parts we hide that need to be seen the most—that need to be reminded they belong and are welcome, too.

As Jen sifted through this story of perfectionism, she started to notice it everywhere. The way she ate perfectly portioned meals, the way she showed up in class a few minutes early, ready to prove how much she knew, the way she kept her apartment spotless, the way she refused to let her naturally curly hair be seen by others after being told it looked messy, the way she refused to receive help in things she didn't already feel competent in . . . so much of her life was dictated by this story, and it stopped her from living into her full, messy, complex, incredible self.

"That need for perfection didn't even come from me," Jen said. "I didn't create that need. Someone else did. I'm just obeying it."

Jen started showing more of her full humanity in our sessions. Instead of editing herself and keeping up her image, she let me in. She stopped trying to impress me. She allowed herself to share her pain instead of her achievements. She gave herself permission to cry without apologizing. She let herself be honest, even when it was hard. She let herself be seen in the mess. "Your mess is good, too," I'd remind her, "you are worthy even in your mistakes." I really validated and honored her messiness as a way of showing her that it was safe to be seen as all of who she was—that I still saw her worth amid all of it. Because I truly did.

In Jen's story, embracing the mess looked like giving herself permission to show up imperfectly, forgiving herself when mistakes inevitably happened, being willing to ask for help when she needed it, allowing herself to be seen in a most honest way, and coming back to the truth that she was good, even in her messiness—just like all of us are.

Jasmine embraced the mess a little differently. For her, it looked like finding the bravery to say no when she needed to say no. It looked like reminding herself over and over that she didn't have to be free of needs in order to be good—just like all of us are. In my story, embracing the mess looks like allowing my uncertainty, grief, doubt, fear, hesitations, mistakes, forgetfulness, and everything I do imperfectly to be okay. It looks like embracing both my professional self and my fully human self. It looks like remembering I'm enough, even when I occasionally forget. And it looks like reminding myself that messiness is a natural part of being human—just like it is for all of us.

I fully believe that embracing the mess has changed my life. When I first began this work, I was so lost, confused, and unsure of what I was doing or why. I thought that this healing journey would lead me on a clear, direct path—instead, it felt more like a maze. But I slowly realized that the point wasn't to reach some final destination or conclusion. The point wasn't to do any of this perfectly, to figure it all out, to find the one thing that would save me or to rush through what is meant to be a lifelong process. The point was to let the messiness be okay.

The practice of embracing the mess takes a sort of surrendering. A loosening of our perceived ideas of control. But when we don't know what's next or what will happen, we open ourselves up to the fact that with uncertainty comes possibility, surprise, and the opportunity for things to go better than we might even believe they could.

Reflections:
- What makes it challenging for you to embrace the messiness of being human?
- What gets in the way of allowing messiness to be okay?
- Whose judgment are you afraid of in relation to accepting the messiness?
- Who do you admire as someone who embraces the messiness fully?
- What would it look like for you to honor the mess a little bit more?
- What might change if messiness became something to honor instead of something to fix?

Affirmations for embracing your humanness:

Your stories don't make you bad;
they make you human.

Your mistakes don't make you bad;
they make you human.

Your messiness doesn't make you
bad; it makes you human.

Your needs don't make you bad;
they make you human.

Your confusion doesn't make you
bad; it makes you human.

Your places in need of healing don't make
you bad; they make you human.

Your humanness doesn't make you
bad; it makes you human.

*You are allowed to embrace your own
humanity. Your humanity is good.*

HONORING OUR FULL SELVES

Discernment Leads to Boundaries

Discernment is about the ability to judge well. A large part of this book has been about discerning what we value and what we want, need, desire, and believe from what we've been taught to value and want, need, desire, and believe; this ongoing work supports us in shifting old stories. But discernment also involves figuring out who to share parts of yourself with, and which parts, and when and how. Who do you share with? Who do you allow to fully witness you? Who do you open your heart to?

Discernment is one of the most crucial practices in honoring and listening to yourself. It's self-trust in practice. As you know, trusting yourself can be incredibly challenging when you might have spent years or even a lifetime tuning out your own voice. It's hard to trust yourself if you were constantly told your thoughts, feelings, or beliefs were wrong.

Discernment becomes more natural as we more easily recognize what works for us and what doesn't, what feels right and what doesn't, what's good for us and what isn't. That, like all things, comes with practice.

Once you've identified the whats, boundaries help keep in the whats you want to welcome into your life, and keep out the whats you don't.

My favorite definition of boundaries was shared by movement facilitator and somatics teacher Prentis Hemphill, who said, "Boundaries are the distance at which I can love you and me simultaneously."

This description of boundaries shows that they are not negative, harsh, or punishing; they allow us to honor ourselves and others at the same time.

Setting boundaries is about being willing to take action and make choices in order to stay in alignment with yourself. Boundaries often include other people, but they aren't for others first; they're for you. We need boundaries with technology, with consumption, with work, with family, with everything. I have boundaries around my phone (not using it before or after a certain time of day; not responding to messages unless I have capacity to; not posting to social media unless it feels good to). I have boundaries around work (not working during hours I don't function best in; not replying to emails on weekends; not taking on more than I can handle). I have boundaries around relationships (spending time with people when it feels good to instead of when it feels obligatory; not forcing friendships that have naturally fizzled; not talking about certain topics with folks who can't do so respectfully). I have boundaries around consumption (not reading every single self-help book there is; not following too many people on social media). These are just a few examples of how boundaries function *for us*. Boundaries are ways to protect our needs, wants, and desires as important and necessary.

In old stories, you might have found it difficult to set boundaries. You might have bent boundaries in order to please others. You might have felt like your needs didn't matter, and therefore, neither did your boundaries. You might have been made to feel guilty about caring for your own needs and creating boundaries that did so. Boundaries are not easy to abide by when we are living in stories of not being enough.

As you heal, grow, and change, though, so do your boundaries. You start knowing boundaries are for you. You start recognizing how boundaries are a way of caring for yourself and living into a new story. Boundaries are not permanent; they are flexible. By allowing them to be flexible, we allow ourselves to repeatedly ask, "What do I have and what do I need? What feels good and what doesn't? What do I have capacity for and what don't I? Where is my energy at and what needs to shift?" It might be to say no. It might be to limit time with someone or something. It might be to refuse to discuss certain topics with certain folks. It might be to limit how much information you consume. It might be to recognize what you do and don't have capacity to hold. Boundaries can look a thousand different ways, and they can be practiced in a thousand different ways.

In my client Jasmine's life, discernment and boundaries took time to implement. She slowly shifted her own story from "I need to be helpful to be worthy" to "I'm worthy as I am." This shift allowed her to choose differently, show up differently, and treat herself differently in the process. Jasmine started noticing what she had capacity for—and what she didn't. She practiced saying no when she needed to say no. She never organized the holiday work party again, but she offered herself compassion when she slipped back into old patterns. Jasmine's implementation of boundaries gave her the freedom she needed to prioritize her own well-being. She finally became the leader of her own life, the champion of her own needs, and the source of affirmation that she had previously sought from others. She reclaimed herself.

Discernment and boundaries will support you in integration by helping you remember what's important to you, keep tabs on what is/isn't working, and create room for more changes as needed. When we implement these aspects of self-tending into our lives, we get to act from our truth. Living from this place is a way of honoring our full humanity and living into our worthiness, goodness, enoughness—our new stories.

Discernment and boundaries

both create space to understand

your wants, needs, and desires

and to make decisions to honor

those wants, needs, and desires.

What do discernment and boundaries look like in daily life?

- Understanding what is good for you, even if it isn't the thing that feels good
- Recognizing what you are and aren't okay with and choosing to act from that space
- Being willing to communicate your needs to others (and to yourself)
- Practicing seeing who can safely meet your needs and who can't
- Honoring your needs, wants, and desires
- Noticing what parts of yourself you share with some but not others
- Being willing to put your own needs first, even if it disappoints someone else
- Allowing yourself to say yes when you want to say yes and no when you want to say no
- Moving from your worthiness instead of moving from old stories
- Listening to yourself and making decisions from what you learn through listening
- Choosing what you need instead of what others want

Some more questions to ask about discernment and boundaries:

- What boundaries need to be in place in order for you to live wholly?
- What boundaries would support you in showing up fully?
- What boundaries would honor your wants, needs, and desires?
- What boundaries would allow you to connect in ways that feel good?

- What boundaries are needed in order for you to live into new stories?
- What boundaries would help you in remembering the truth of who you are?

Consumption Leads to Action

Boundaries are not just about keeping things out; they also include what we let in. Something that I find important to explore is what we're consuming and whether or not it is supporting us—whether our consumption is helping or harming. In this day and age, so many of us are constantly consuming information about personal growth. "Self-help" and therapy and coaching and Instagram and podcasts and books can easily and quickly become another way of avoiding actually doing the work. You can continue consuming information and never act, which keeps you stuck in the belief that you can't change. Constantly consuming can also reinforce the idea that others know better than you do or that others have it more figured out than you do. In other words, it can reinforce old stories of being inadequate or not enough.

When we have a plethora of information but take no action to integrate that information, it becomes very easy to judge ourselves. It can also keep us from feeling like we're capable at all, always moving the "finish line" further and further away. This is where consumption can be detrimental to living into new stories. I think a lot about how writing this book is, in a way, contributing to the culture of feeling like you need another perspective or the perfect practices in order to finally feel better. My hope is that it's the kind of consumption that encourages compassion, integration, understanding, and action.

If you are reading this book, I would imagine you are someone who engages in this kind of work. You've most likely done some of it already. You might know which parts of yourself still need healing and tenderness. You probably have some awareness around the tools that have worked for you and those that haven't. And . . . I would also guess that you've found it difficult to get started. At least I've felt this way.

Living into new stories requires making the conscious effort to practice the tools you read about daily. That effort is at the heart of the shift from feeling unworthy of change to knowing change is possible. Even before we fully believe it, we must practice it. When we do, new stories slowly feel more true and real. We begin to realize we do deserve our healing, we are worthy of our healing, and we are capable of our healing.

Integration is where many people get stuck, including me. Some days it feels easy and good; other days it feels impossible and exhausting. We can read about mindfulness and mistake it for actually practicing mindfulness. We can explore content about self-compassion but forget to practice it with ourselves. We can assume we need the next trendy healing modality before fully utilizing all the modalities we already know. Sometimes we might not even want to act from wholeness—it might feel easier to let it all go and return to old ways of being. Knowing that these moments will happen ahead of time allows us to respond to those feelings with compassion instead of using them as reasons to stop caring for ourselves in the ways we know we can. I see this in clients, too—the resistance to continuing integration when it gets challenging or when it feels uncomfortable. As I shared earlier, resistance is part of change. It's so understandable, and when we keep showing up for ourselves anyway, we start recognizing our own resiliency and capability.

What is your relationship with consumption like? How do you know when you're consuming too much? How is what you're consuming supporting you in integrating new stories? Checking in with

Consumption:	Action:
Learning about mindfulness	Practicing mindfulness
Reading about self-compassion	Practicing self-compassion
Understanding boundaries	Implementing boundaries
Buying another self-help or personal development book	Practicing what you already know within you
Gaining more knowledge	Engaging in aligned action

yourself regularly around this allows you to notice your patterns and shift what isn't working.

Vulnerability Leads to Connection

Sharing my story has been one of the biggest contributing factors to my healing journey. I spent most of my life keeping a lot of my feelings, emotions, and thoughts to myself; being able to express my truth to others has allowed me to reckon with my own story, as well as create the stories I want to carry. There is potent medicine that comes from being witnessed in this way, but deep vulnerability is required to be fully seen.

Sharing my story didn't start with sharing it on Instagram or in a book or telling everyone; it started with my therapist. It started small. I was honest about all the complexities and nuances and details of my story, with one curious witness. It started with slowly, gently, and thoughtfully discerning what I was ready to share and what I wasn't yet ready to release. Then, gradually, I started sharing with a few close friends. I started sharing with smaller groups of people. I then shared part of my story with my journalism class in junior college, which led to sharing parts of my story on the front page of a newspaper. I later shared more parts of my story in the class at UC Santa Cruz. As my sharing expanded, my capacity to be witnessed and to witness myself grew, too. This happened over a period of twenty years, and it continues to unfold as I do.

This is what it means to be vulnerable. Brené Brown, whose work on this topic has changed my life and the lives of many, defines vulnerability as uncertainty, risk, and emotional exposure. In other words, vulnerability requires us to show up and be seen, even when we can't control the outcome. This is why it's so important to find people and places who honor us—so we can share safely.

We cannot fully show up in our lives if we don't practice vulnerability, little by little and step by step. It allows our full selves to see and be seen, to hear and be heard. Vulnerability is a lifeline from one human heart to another—an invisible cord that ties us all together in some way. Where it gets tricky is if we feel pressured to be vulnerable before we're ready, with people who don't feel safe, or in spaces that don't honor all of who we are. In the world of social media, especially, there is an unspoken pressure to be "#authentic," and for many, this means sharing their story. It's inspiring and incredible to witness how many people are choosing to speak honestly about their experiences. But know that you never *have* to share your story that way; vulnerability doesn't look the same for all of us. For some, it means sharing what has happened to them in order to find healing; for others, it might mean opening up with a few friends or a therapist and feeling that is enough. And for others, it might just look like sharing the real, full *you*. True vulnerability requires that we tune inward and ask ourselves why we are sharing, whether it's safe to share, and what we hope to get from sharing. From here, we can determine how we can share our stories (or ourselves) in a way that supports our healing.

One way I empower clients is to remind them that they get to choose what they share. They get to choose what feels safe and what doesn't, what feels right and what doesn't. This is true for all of us— we get to choose. Reminding yourself that it is your choice often makes it feel safer to practice vulnerability in a genuine way, rather than in a performative or forced way.

When you imagine sharing your story, as well as sharing the new stories you are creating and cultivating, I encourage you to explore the people who feel the safest to do that with. It might be your therapist. It might be a family member, at a small family gathering. It might be one of your friends who holds space for you. It might be a lot of people. We each have our own capacity for vulnerability and our own range for what feels safe, so exploring what it looks like within yourself is really important.

Questions I might ask myself before sharing something privately:
- Do I trust this person to hold space for me?
- Do I feel safe with this person?
- Do I feel comfortable with this person knowing this about me?
- Have I had positive and supportive experiences sharing with this person before?
- Does this person still love me even in my depths, pain, and mistakes?
- Am I able to be my full self around this person?
- Would it feel better to share with this person than not to?

Questions I might ask myself before sharing something publicly:
- Is this a scar or a wound? (Glennon Doyle wrote about the distinction between a scar and a wound as a way of discerning what is safe and potentially unsafe to share—a scar meaning you've done enough healing to share confidently, and a wound meaning you're still healing and perhaps not quite ready to share.)
- Am I sharing to prove something or to connect?
- Will I be okay with sharing this, regardless of what the outcome is?
- Am I okay with receiving criticism or judgment from sharing this?
- Is there a greater message or universal theme in what I'm sharing?

- Do I feel good about sharing this? Does it offer me something healing?
- Am I okay with anyone and everyone knowing this about me?

Different Methods of Sharing Your Story

Speaking our stories out loud is wildly powerful, but there are other ways to explore and express our stories and ourselves. Writing is a practice that brings immense insight for me. There are methods that each of us can implement depending on what works for us, what we enjoy, and what brings us meaning.

Whatever sharing might look like for you, I encourage you to try it. Explore ways of being witnessed. Be willing to be seen in all of who you are—not just the pretty, together, admirable parts but the harder parts, too, and the parts that you may have hidden. Be willing to be seen as your full self. I encourage you to discover spaces, places, and people you feel can hold you with the tenderness and grace you deserve. As I've shared before, we cannot do this work of being human alone. We cannot get through life hiding ourselves and expect to feel seen. We need each other.

Other ways to explore your story:

- Art of all kinds

- Music, song, and voice

- Collaboration, connection, and sharing

- Therapy, coaching, or mentorship

- Connecting with nature

- Any kind of creativity

- Writing poetry, letters, and prose

- Movement, dance, and yoga

- What would you add?

BRINGING IT ALL TOGETHER

Finding Self-acceptance

One of my heroes, the humanistic psychologist Carl Rogers, said one of my favorite quotes. I've mentioned it before, but it bears repeating: "The curious paradox is that when I accept myself as I am, then I can change." Have you ever experienced this—that things start feeling a bit easier right when you accept them?

"How do I accept all of myself when I don't like all of myself?" I've asked this question over and over in my own therapy, and it has been asked of me over and over in therapy. It feels paradoxical to accept what we don't like. And, as paradoxical as it sounds, I think it's the whole point of all this inner work we do—to find acceptance in all of it. To know that you don't need to love all of yourself, all of the time, in order to know that you're enough. To know that you never need to have it all figured out in order to be enough.

The thing is, acceptance doesn't necessarily mean we like all parts of ourselves. It means opening our arms to what is instead of pushing it away, denying it, or pretending like it isn't. It means embracing the imperfection, the confusion, the messiness, the joy, the pain, the presence, the distraction, the beauty, the fear . . . embracing all of it for what it is, *whenever* it is. Self-acceptance is a lifelong process, and it's one that I have found naturally develops as we do the work of understanding, reframing, and integrating our stories.

To me, self-acceptance is the culmination of doing the work of getting honest, getting brave, and getting free. Awareness of our stories leads to the understanding needed to shift them. Shifting them leads to the ability to live into integrity. Living into integrity leads to (hopefully) finding acceptance in the whole of who we are, including who we once were. It allows us to embrace who we've been, who we are, and who we're becoming.

We so easily forget that accepting ourselves isn't about reaching some final destination but is more about doing the deep work of slowing down, turning inward, and gently reintroducing yourself to parts of you that you were told you should fix. The stories you learned to believe might have made you think you needed to hide, be ashamed of, erase, or minimize certain parts of who you are. They might have caused you to pretend, to put on masks, to mold yourself to others' expectations, or to stop seeing how amazing all of your qualities and quirks make you. When we reintroduce these parts of us as just that—parts of us—we get to create new relationships with those parts. We get to accept all of who we are instead of hiding parts of us. We get to embrace our full humanity instead of incessantly trying to fix it. The point of healing is to accept who we are and live into our wholeness. To come home to ourselves. To return to who we are. It's exactly what you've been doing as you move through this book.

We don't need to get rid of what's hard. We don't need to eliminate the pain, hide from the hurt, or push away the stories we once carried. Instead, we need to allow ourselves the chance to show up as our whole self. To remember we've always been whole. To remember we're already enough.

All the practices, mindsets, and reminders in this book are meant to support you in remembering your wholeness. My hope is you are beginning to witness what is possible within you—that you are approaching an opening—that you are realizing your limitlessness.

Unraveling our hard stories is deeply confronting. It invites guilt, shame, and self-judgment to come to the surface easily. It causes us to question why we did certain things, how certain patterns came to be, and how we've grown into who we are. In our culture, we are often taught to feel a sense of shame about the ways we've shown up in the past. But I don't think we should.

In order to move past shame over and over, I've had to learn to fully accept all of who I am, all of the stories I've held closely, all the things I've said that I wish I could take back, all the times I fall back into old habits that don't serve me . . . all of it. Living into our wholeness requires us to make space for *all* parts of us. Self-acceptance requires us to accept *all* parts of us, including the parts we're still healing.

This, I think, is the whole point: finding and developing the capacity to hold the fluidity, the complexity, the bigness of who we are. It's the point of examining our stories, it's the point of doing the work of reframing and unlearning, and it's the point of integrating new stories—to make space for all of who we've been, all of who we are, and all of who we're becoming and unbecoming.

Finding Meaning and Purpose

When I applied to graduate school to become a therapist, I was afraid my old stories would hold me back. I was afraid they would make me look weak or incapable in my classes and that they would make me appear less professional in my practice. I applied anyway, but those fears were applying with me.

A few weeks after turning in my application, I got an email inviting me to an in-person interview. I was equally elated and terrified. Writing about myself and my dreams was one thing, but going and talking to someone face-to-face? That was another mountain to climb. My anxiety rose as the day came closer.

On the day of my interview, I parked at the campus of Dominican

How self-acceptance
shows up in our lives:

- Embracing pain instead of running from it

- Honoring what is instead of hiding from it

- Allowing your messiness to be okay

- Validating your complexities and vastness

- Not beating yourself up when you mess up

- Being with what is before trying to change it

- Nurturing who you are as you are

- Accepting your past without self-punishment

- Engaging in the present moment fully

- Forgiving yourself, over and over again

University of California and sat in my car for a few moments. My anxiety, by then, was at its peak. My heart was beating fast. I reminded myself, "This doesn't define you either way. Just be you." I walked into the building, let them know I'd arrived, and waited for my interviewer to greet me.

A man came down and introduced himself. Even with his friendly demeanor, I was immediately intimidated. I had planned what I was going to say in response to certain questions. I'd planned to share about my professional experience and the knowledge I had gained so far in my studies. I'd planned not to address the personal parts of my application essay. As we walked upstairs to a large conference room and started talking, this plan quickly went out the window.

He asked me why I wanted to become a therapist. Instead of talking about the courses I had taken and the group home I worked at, I talked about what I had learned from my own experiences. I talked about how being an adoptee allowed me to more deeply understand what it was like to carry a story of never-enoughness. I shared about my history with depression and how it gave me deeper empathy for those who were moving through their own stories. I talked about how important being seen and heard was in my own healing and how meaningful it was to see and hear others. I was just myself.

At the end of our interview, he said, "Congratulations." I was accepted on the spot.

The meaning I had made from my pain gave me purpose to show up more fully in the world. The meaning I had made from healing gave me purpose to navigate ways I could support others in finding healing, too. That is what inspired me to become a therapist. Not the grades I got in undergraduate school or the classes I took but the life I had lived and the people I connected with along the way. As it turns out, it wasn't something I needed to be ashamed of but was something I could share proudly.

I realized my purpose when I was my full self. When I accepted my full self. I realized that my purpose was to just *be* my full self.

Finding meaning and purpose from our path, our stories, our experiences, and our life gives us the motivation needed to keep integrating—to keep healing. Not everything happens for a reason. Not everything has meaning. But when we can infuse our lives by transforming our pain into something more than just pain . . . when we can use our hurts for more than serving old stories . . . we can create something beautiful from what started as total darkness. We can alchemize what was once just hard into something more. We can create new meaning from the stories we once carried while we live into our fullness.

Questions to ask about meaning and purpose:
- When you think of applying meaning to who you've been and who you are becoming, what words come to mind? What feelings arise?
- How might meaning and purpose be infused into the life you are creating? Where can you tap into your purpose as a way of showing up more fully?
- How have the stories you've carried guided you to who you actually are?
- How have your experiences supported the understanding and wisdom you now hold?
- What might you do with your wisdom and the meaning you've made in order to live into purpose, on purpose?

Be More You

Here you are. Notice how it feels to have gotten this far in the book. Notice what has made its way within you, what you're left questioning, what you know more deeply, and what you want to explore more fully. Notice where you feel a little lighter and where you might have cleared the way for something new to take place. Notice how it has felt to spend a little time getting to know yourself more intimately.

With understanding, reframing mindsets, integration practices, and new ways of showing up in the world, I want to remind you that the biggest invitation of this book is to be more you. Healing allows us to become more ourselves—to become our full selves—and I truly can't think of anything more freeing than that.

When you think about being more you, I invite you to consider:
- What needs have shifted? What desires are asking to be noticed?
- How do you hope to feel each day? What will help get you there?
- What do you hold as a vision for your future that didn't seem possible from your old stories and beliefs?
- How can the stories you are living into support you in creating that future?
- What does it feel like to imagine showing up more you?

The world doesn't need us to diminish ourselves anymore. It doesn't need us to silence our brilliance or minimize our gifts. It doesn't need us to go along with what isn't working. It doesn't need us to feel broken. It doesn't need us to feel not enough.

Being *more you* enriches not only your

own life; it enriches the world, too.

It enriches all of us.

The world needs us to trust our goodness. To know our enoughness. To live into our worthiness. To honor all we are and to recognize the unique gifts and contributions we have to offer. To make room for play, joy, and ease. To connect authentically and vulnerably. To let our full humanity be okay—and to let that of others be okay, too. This is what the world needs.

Being more you not only enriches your own life, it enriches the world. It enriches all of us.

Change Starts with You, in More Ways Than One

Most of this book has been about inner work, our personal experiences, and how to hold ourselves in the exploration and shifting of our own stories. A powerful outcome of doing this work is that we grow our capacity to live into new stories not only within ourselves but within our relationships, our communities, and the world. When we have a deeper sense of our worth, our goodness, and our enoughness, we have a greater capacity to see and witness that in others. When we move from a place of wholeness, we believe in change and have more capacity to invoke change, be fierce about what matters to us, and find the fortitude to take action within and outside of ourselves. It's much easier to speak your truth when you're doing so from a place of self-knowing. It's much easier to discern what actions you want to take in the world when you're willing to mess up. It's much easier to see the goodness in others when you're able to see it in yourself. The false stories are no longer in the way. The programming is no longer running the show. The proving or hiding is no longer impeding our ability to connect with others. The need to be liked is no longer stopping us from speaking up. The belief in our own belonging allows us to want others to belong, too. Living from your enoughness changes everything.

Until I accepted myself, I wasn't able to fully show up in the world. Shifting my inner world has given me a chance to respond to the world around me with more compassion, grace, presence, and willingness to get it wrong. That, in turn, has allowed me to fully witness injustice, to champion causes I care about, to take action from a place of integrity instead of a place of shame, guilt, or fear. I am now able to share my thoughts and insights more widely, knowing I will mess up sometimes. I'm able to have conversations about racism and other social issues, knowing I may get called out or given feedback sometimes. I'm able to show up fully because I know I have my own back. My inner work has allowed me to be a better partner, friend, guide, community member, and fellow citizen.

Imagine what the world would look like if every individual went through the process of understanding, reframing, and integrating their stories into their lives; if they modeled this for their children; if their children modeled it for their children.

Some of the shifts that are possible when we begin moving from a place of understanding:

- We more clearly see injustice and systemic harm
- We have more recognition of power differentials, cultural narratives, and inequity
- We have more space to unhook from harmful collective programming
- We live into our values, morals, and beliefs with more conviction
- We more readily take action toward what we care about
- We take responsibility for harm we cause and own our behavior rather than spiral into shame
- We help from a place of fullness instead of a place of proving
- We do deeper, more honest, more impactful work

- We recognize ourselves in one another, which creates more empathy and compassion
- We relate to others from a sense of connectedness and common humanity
- We develop healthier, more sound relationships
- We're better able to care for ourselves and each other
- We're better able to respond rather than react
- We're more willing to get it wrong and try again next time
- We expand our capacity for growth, change, and evolution

As you continue integrating new stories, beliefs, and ways of being with yourself into the various parts of your life, I encourage you to notice what else shifts—how your relationships change, how your approach to work changes, how your ability to show up for the causes you believe in changes, and how your approach to your community evolves. Moving from your new story helps you live into your purpose, which naturally affects your relationship with all parts of yourself, with others, and with the world.

With this in mind, I invite you to explore the world you want to live in. Now that you know your ability to shift your own inner stories, what shifts would you like to see outside of you? What do you envision for a more just, connected, and beautiful world? What changes do you hope to be a part of? What causes do you hope to push further along? What shifts would be a reflection of your own worthiness, goodness, enoughness?

The world needs more humans who are showing up from their whole self. The world needs more humans who are in touch with all parts of who they are. The world needs more humans who are willing to accept their full humanity and are willing to see the humanity in those who differ from them. The world needs more humans who aren't afraid to fail, aren't afraid to be wrong, and aren't afraid to make mistakes. The world needs more humans who understand, shift, and choose the stories they tell themselves.

The deeper I understand, shift, choose, and embody my own story of enoughness, the deeper my work in the world becomes. The wider my self-acceptance grows, the wider my acceptance of other people grows. The more room I give myself to make mistakes and still be good, the more room I also hold for others to do the same. The more in touch I am with my truth, the more I'm willing to see the truth of what is happening around me. I am constantly reminded of how we mirror to one another what we see in ourselves; doing this work of claiming our own stories is wildly powerful not just within our own experience but also in the context in which we live. We become more clear mirrors to others; what matters to us becomes more obvious; the next right move feels slightly less intimidating; and our ability to live a life of purpose, intention, devotion, and meaning widens exponentially.

Carrying Your Stories Forward, for Yourself and for the World

In the writing process for this book, I have naturally been reflecting deeply on what it means to heal, to understand and integrate our stories, and to make room for new ones.

One thing that stands out while I explore these themes is how much hope I have for what is possible. How much hope I have for our capacity to change, to grow and transform, to heal. How much hope I have for our ability to choose stories that help us, rather than ones that harm us. How much hope I have for our innate striving toward wholeness. How much hope I have for all humans of all backgrounds to eventually realize they don't have to do any of this alone. I have so much hope for me, for you, and for all of us, even when I (or we) forget it sometimes.

I hope you've been able to see that healing, shifting our stories, and living fully as ourselves isn't about following a 1-2-3 step process, or doing it "right" all the time, or forcing it, or expecting it to look the same for you as it does for others. I hope you've been able to see that it's a process—a practice—one that you will return to again and again throughout your life. I've shared a lot of myself in this book because speaking from my own experience is really the best tool I have as a writer and teacher, but I hope you've also seen yourself in what I've shared. I hope you've been able to imagine a new possibility of being with yourself—a new way of carrying your experiences—a new way of honoring all of who you are. I've been thinking of you every step of the way as I write, imagining talking with you about these things, and envisioning the way these words might seep into you or connect with you. You've been with me the whole way.

As you put down this book, and as we move forward with both the stories we've worked to unravel and the stories we are in the process of rewriting, there are some truths I want to leave you with. These are truths I share often, truths I revisit myself when I need them. These are truths that support me in continuing to hope, even when things get tough (because they will).

1. We cannot control what has happened to us or how we've responded in the past. What we can do is gain a deeper understanding of what has happened and how it has affected us, recognize our power in holding space for it, allow ourselves to receive the help and support we deserve, and honor our ability to move forward in more compassionate ways. May we continue exploring.

2. Our worth, goodness, and enoughness are right here within us, right now. They have been since we came to be. The stories we created and the stories we were told about ourselves might have hidden our innate wholeness from us, and yet here it is, waiting to be remembered. May we continue remembering who we are.

3. When we heal, shift, grow, change, and transform, we are not becoming better; we are simply returning to what we have always been. As you uncover what you may feel are new strengths, beliefs, and discoveries about yourself, I invite you to remember that those aren't new. They've always been there, and what a gift it is to do the work of uncovering them. May we continue returning to ourselves.

4. Needing other people is not a sign of weakness but a sign of our humanity. We (all of us) are born needing others, and we will always need others. It's okay to need help, to need support, to need connection, and to need to be seen. You were born to need these things, and you deserve these things. May we continue connecting.

5. Wounded people wound people. Those who hurt us are carrying their own hurt. We can empathize with others while also being willing to do what we need to take care of ourselves and our needs. We can understand how others' stories impact them while also honoring our own needs. May we continue holding boundaries while also holding compassion.

6. Mindfulness, curiosity, self-compassion, and aligned action are ways of being that allow us to see ourselves and others clearly. Practicing these mindsets is one of the most impactful ways to honor ourselves and others, to live with presence, and to create enough space for what's possible to unfold and be found. May we continue practicing.

7. Our stories can keep us stagnant, or they can allow us to soar. When we rewrite our stories and practice living into them, we start being

able to create what works for us and part with what doesn't. We start soaring. May we continue choosing.

8. Making room for our own stories allows us to make room for the stories of others. Experiencing the shift of our own stories allows us to realize others are capable of shifting theirs, too. Our stories ripple out into our community in so many ways. May we continue witnessing.

9. It is never too late to begin the work of understanding, reframing, and integrating your story. It is never too late to start over. It is never too late to create a new story. It is never too late to heal. It is never too late. May we continue learning and unlearning.

10. Showing up for all the parts of you that you at one time didn't know how to show up for is one of the most beautiful and potent acts of healing I can think of, and you are doing it by reading this book. May we continue showing up for our full humanity.

As you move into the world and deeper into yourself, I encourage you to keep reflecting. Keep asking questions. Keep exploring. Keep digging. Keep tending. Keep uprooting. Keep learning and unlearning. Keep allowing yourself to receive support. Keep staying curious. Keep forgiving yourself. Keep getting to know yourself. Keep listening. Keep honoring. Keep editing. Keep shifting. Keep changing. Keep allowing. Keep creating a more and more loving home within you, for you. Keep going.

It has been a gift to share with you, to teach some of what I've learned, and to remind you that we can often find a lot more in the questions than in the answers. My story continues alongside you, ever evolving and ever changing. May we remember our capacity to shift, pivot, reframe and rewrite, heal, grow, change, and transform, over and over. I honor your resiliency and your willingness to dive deeper into yourself. I honor your capacity to grow, change, and transform, over and over, in whatever ways you want or need to. I honor your overcoming. I honor your process. I honor your deep worthiness, goodness, and enoughness. I honor your stories and your healing. I honor all of you, and I hope you honor all of you, too. Cheers to the next chapter—to having the final say in how our story goes.

Ten Steps to BS

A ten-step guide to calling BS (bogus story) on your own stories:

1. Notice the story that arises. Feel into what's happening within your body. Feel the sensations.
2. Name it: "The story I'm telling myself is . . ." (thank you to Brené Brown for sharing this prompt frequently)
3. Get curious around what that story does for you, how it serves you, how it keeps you safe or protects you.
4. Thank yourself for creating the stories you once needed to feel safe in the world.
5. With compassion, ask yourself if this is a story you want to keep carrying.
6. If it is, don't read steps 6 through 10, and carry on.
7. If it's not, use your innate creativity to formulate a new story that feels supportive, expansive, and kind.
8. Tell yourself the new story, over and over, even if you don't believe it at first.
9. Start telling other people the story, too. Let others hold it with you and reflect it back to you.
10. Notice what it feels like to live from *that* place—to take an active role in your own story.

Repeat.

Resource Guide

Since a book cannot possibly cover the vastness of healing, growth, and reclaiming our stories, I've created a short list of resources with some of my recommendations for other places to find support on this journey of inner work and coming home to ourselves. There are so many beyond these, too!

BOOKS

Trauma:

The Body Keeps the Score by Bessel van der Kolk

The Polyvagal Theory by Stephen Porges

Waking the Tiger by Peter Levine

The Politics of Trauma by Staci K. Haines

It Didn't Start with You by Mark Wolynn

Trauma-Sensitive Mindfulness by David Treleaven

The Boy Who Was Raised as a Dog by Bruce Perry

Connection:

How to Be an Adult in Relationships by David Richo

Conscious Loving: The Journey to Co-commitment by Gay Hendricks and Kathlyn Hendricks

Nonviolent Communication by Marshall Rosenberg
Hold Me Tight by Sue Johnson
Attached by Amir Levine and Rachel S. F. Heller

Personal Growth:
Anything by Brené Brown (seriously anything)
Radical Acceptance by Tara Brach
When Things Fall Apart by Pema Chödrön
Self-Compassion by Kristin Neff
Resilient by Rick Hanson with Forrest Hanson
Burnout by Emily Nagoski and Amelia Nagoski
The Untethered Soul by Michael A. Singer
Untamed by Glennon Doyle
How to Not Always Be Working by Marlee Grace
Emotional Intelligence by Daniel Goleman

Therapeutic Workbooks:
The Mindful Self-Compassion Workbook by Kristin Neff and
    Christopher Germer
The Inner Child Workbook by Cathyn L. Taylor
The Mindfulness and Acceptance Workbook for Stress Reduction

Soul Nourishment:
Anything by Mary Oliver
All About Love by bell hooks
Emergent Strategy by adrienne maree brown
After the Rain by Alexandra Elle
Belonging by Toko-pa Turner
Big Magic by Elizabeth Gilbert
Women Who Run with the Wolves by Clarissa Pinkola Estés
The Artist's Way by Julia Cameron

(Narrowing down a book list is honestly one of the hardest parts of creating this book!)

PODCASTS

Tara Brach Podcast: enlightening and nourishing talks on self-compassion and acceptance

Hey Girl: Alex Elle's conversations with women around self-care and healing

On Being with Krista Tippet: spiritually resonant conversations about humanity

Unlocking Us with Brené Brown: Brené Brown interviews special humans about being human

Everything Belongs with Madison Morrigan: real, meaningful conversations about living into who we are

Hurry Slowly: conversations about finding more presence and slowing down

Needy: Mara Glatzel's podcast about honoring our needs and caring for ourselves fully

Where Should We Begin? with Esther Perel: therapist Esther Perel sharing couples therapy sessions

HOW TO FIND A THERAPIST

Psychology Today (www.psychologytody.com): enter your zip code and preferences to find a therapist near you

Google therapists in your area and see if their websites/work resonate with you

Check out therapists on social media to get a feel for their style

Ask people you know for referrals and recommendations

Check out Open Path Collective (openpathcollective.org) if lower-fee services are needed

Get a referral from your PCP

Utilize your insurance company and find someone on their list

TEACHERS, MENTORS, AND CREATIVES
FROM ALL SECTORS WHO HAVE INFORMED
MY WORK AND TAUGHT ME SO MUCH:

Desiree Adaway

Maya Angelou

Sarah Blondin

Hiro Boga

Tara Brach

adrienne maree brown

Brené Brown

Julia Cameron

Pema Chödrön

Ram Dass

Lalah Delia

Joan Didion

Glennon Doyle

Alexandra Elle

Diana Fosha

Chris Gerber

Elizabeth Gilbert

Paul Gilbert

John and Julie Gottman

Thích Nhất Hạnh

Rick Hanson

Steven Hayes

Tricia Hersey

bell hooks

Sue Johnson

Jack Kornfield

Anne Lamott

Gabor Maté

Jennifer Mullan

Mary Oliver

Rachel Ricketts

Carl Rogers

Sharon Salzberg

Richard Schwartz

Dani Shapiro

Dan Siegel

Rebecca Solnit

Cheryl Strayed

Sonya Renee Taylor

Krista Tippett

Toko-pa Turner

Francis Weller

Michael White

Irvin Yalom

. . . and the countless humans not on this list but still very much inspiring me, my work, and my life.

My Deep Gratitude

Writing this book has at times been such a solitary process and, at the very same time, it has been one informed and nurtured by the support, love, inspiration, guidance, and care from so many people, near and far.

To my agent, Laura Lee Mattingly: Thank you for seeing something in me from the beginning, for your fierce advocacy, and for encouraging me to write this book in a way that feels right and true for me.

To my editor, Emily Graff: Your belief in my voice, my story, and my work has shaped this book greatly. Thank you for your incredible support, and for becoming not just an editor but a friend over the last few years.

To my team at Simon & Schuster: Thank you for your creative vision, for your support in moving through edits after edits, and for having faith in the mission and purpose of this book.

To my professors, mentors, and supervisors over the years: Thank you for expanding my beliefs, nurturing my passions, and for showing me the gift of learning and growing, both personally and professionally.

To my teachers from afar: You've taught me so much about what it means to be human, and I carry the wisdom I've learned from you everywhere I go.

To my many therapists and guides over the last two decades: I'm not sure where I would be without the gentle care I felt on your couches and in your circles. Being seen by you shaped me.

To my colleagues, coworkers, and peers over the years: I am endlessly inspired by your tenacity, compassion, and capacity to see the good in people. The world is better because of you.

To the clients I've been lucky enough to work with: I am awed by you and have learned just as much from you as you may have learned from therapy.

To my friends, past and present, near and far: Thank you for seeing me, for making me laugh, for your deep connection and for making my life brighter. I love you.

To my big, weird, wonderful family: I wouldn't be me without any of you, and I'm so thankful for my continuously expanding family tree. Each of you is a part of me.

To my husband, Thomas: Your partnership, cheesy puns, nurturance, and endless support is something I am grateful for every single day. With you, I am both anchored and free. Thank you for never failing to remind me that I am already enough in moments I forget.

Index

embodiment, 11, 169–70, 212

emotions, 6, 8, 17, 182, 196

and becoming aware of stories,
42, 53, 66–67, 71–72, 81

reframing stories and, 93, 105,
113, 118, 122, 124, 135,
152–53

understanding stories and,
23–24, 27–28, 38

empathy, 5, 17, 71

bringing it all together and, 205,
211, 214

reframing stories and, 121, 126

employment, 189, 211

and becoming aware of stories,
56, 66, 79, 81

reframing stories and, 134, 141,
146, 153

understanding stories and,
36–38, 40

empowerment, *see* power
empowerment

enoughness, 3–11

and becoming aware of stories,
41, 43–56, 59, 61–63,
79–81

bringing it all together and,
201–2, 205, 207–9, 211–12,
214, 216

honoring full selves and, 189–90,
193, 197–98

integrating stories and, 169–71,
173, 175–78, 182, 184

Olivera's story and, 3–4, 6–7, 9,
20, 33–36, 46, 61, 63, 79, 94,
112, 119–20, 127–29, 161,
169, 178, 205, 212

reframing stories and, 88, 90–91,
94, 101, 112, 118–21, 125,
127–30, 133, 153–54, 161,
164

understanding stories and, 30,
33–36

environment, 15–16

and becoming aware of stories,
48, 57, 68, 75–76, 81

reframing stories and, 95–96,
103

understanding stories and, 23,
25–26, 28–30

eye movement desensitization
therapy (EMDR), 97

failure, 23

and becoming aware of stories,
43–44, 54–55, 58

bringing it all together and,
211–12

integrating stories and, 173, 184

reframing stories and, 98, 117

families, 3–6

and becoming aware of stories,
45–48, 50, 54, 57, 61, 67–70,
78, 81

honoring full selves and, 189,
197

reframing stories and, 90, 93,
95–137, 141, 143–46,
148–57, 165
understanding stories and, 21,
23–25, 29, 36–38
surrender, 149, 186
in compassion, 126–27
what it might look like, 127

Taylor, Jill Bolte, 23
Taylor, Sonya Renee, 18*n*, 31, 158
therapy, 13, 19
and becoming aware of stories,
48, 51, 53, 63, 67, 69–72, 74,
80–81
bringing it all together and, 201,
203–5
honoring full selves and, 193,
196–97, 200
Olivera's story and, 4–6, 67,
69–70, 120–23, 151, 196,
203–5
reframing stories and, 97–98,
120–23, 128, 151, 156, 163
understanding stories and, 36–40
trauma, 13, 29*n*, 49, 106*n*
reframing stories and, 95, 97
understanding stories and,
26–28
Treleaven, David, 106*n*
trust, 155, 173, 209
and becoming aware of stories,
49, 54–55, 57–58, 79

in curiosity, 116–17
honoring full selves and, 188,
198
Olivera's story and, 49, 79,
116–17, 161
reframing stories and, 96, 104,
116–17, 124, 126–27, 130,
136, 149, 161
understanding stories and, 34–35

uncertainty, *see* certainty,
uncertainty

validation, 16, 35, 185, 204
and becoming aware of stories,
69–73
Olivera's story and, 69–70,
116–17, 151
reframing stories and, 116–17,
122, 137–40, 150–51
what it might look like, 71
values, 16, 188, 210
and becoming aware of stories,
48, 54, 56
examples of, 155
exploration of, 129, 154–57
reframing stories and, 88, 120,
129, 148, 150, 154–57
understanding stories and, 24,
27–28, 31
van der Kolk, Bessel, 28, 95
vulnerability, 5, 37, 209
in leading to connection, 196–99

About the Author

LISA OLIVERA is a writer, therapist, and creative who shares work centered around radical acceptance, cultivating compassion, integrating our stories, and embracing our full humanity. She holds a master's degree in counseling and psychology and has worked in schools, community-based mental health, and private practice. Lisa's work and writing has appeared in many publications, including the *New York Times*, the *Guardian*, the *Huffington Post*, and *Good Morning America*. She lives with her husband and daughter in Northern California.